Investing in the Future: Harnessing Private Capital Flows for Environmentally Sustainable Development

HILARY F. FRENCH

Payal Sampat, *Staff Researcher*

Jane A. Peterson, *Editor*

WORLDWATCH PAPER 139
February 1998

FINANCIAL SUPPORT for the Institute is provided by the Geraldine R. Dodge Foundation, the Ford Foundation, the Foundation for Ecology and Development, the William and Flora Hewlett Foundation, W. Alton Jones Foundation, John D. and Catherine T. MacArthur Foundation, Charles Stewart Mott Foundation, the Curtis and Edith Munson Foundation, David and Lucille Packard Foundation, Rasmussen Foundation, Rockefeller Brothers Fund, Rockefeller Financial Services, Summit Foundation, Surdna Foundation, Turner Foundation, U.N. Population Fund, Wallace Genetic Foundation, Wallace Global Fund, Weeden Foundation, and the Winslow Foundation.

Table of Contents

ACKNOWLEDGMENTS: I am grateful to many individuals for commenting on preliminary drafts of this paper, as well as for supplying data and information. They include: Michelle Chan-Fishel, Riva Krut, Lisa Fernandez, Masataka Fujita, Ray Mataloni, Carmini Luther Michelitsch, David Schorr, Frances Seymour, David Smith, and Frederik van Bolhuis. Many of my Worldwatch colleagues reviewed the manuscript and provided useful input, including Richard Bell, Christopher Flavin, Michael Renner, and David Roodman. Thanks also to Payal Sampat for her invaluable help with research; Jane Peterson for her skillful editing; and Lori Ann Brown, Mary Caron, Suzanne Clift, Laura Malinowski, and Amy Warehime for their assistance at various stages of the production and outreach process.

HILARY F. FRENCH is Vice President for Research at the Worldwatch Institute. Her research and writing center on two main areas: the integration of environmental concerns into international economic policy, and the role of international institutions in environmental protection and sustainable development. She is the author of six Worldwatch Papers, including Worldwatch Paper 126, *Partnership for the Planet: An Environmental Agenda for the United Nations,* and Worldwatch Paper 113, *Costly Tradeoffs: Reconciling Trade and the Environment.* She is co-author of eight of the Institute's annual *State of the World* reports, among other publications. She holds degrees from Dartmouth College and from the Fletcher School of Law and Diplomacy.

Introduction

Nineteen ninety-seven was a rough year for the global economy. As a wave of currency depreciations, stock market collapses, and bank closures swept through East Asia, economists who just months earlier were singing the praises of the "Asian miracle" were suddenly decrying the region's weak economic underpinnings. While these countries reeled from the crisis, an ecological calamity hit: some 2 million hectares of Indonesian rain forest were consumed by massive fires, blanketing large parts of Southeast Asia in a health-threatening haze that sent thousands of people to hospitals and shut down schools and businesses, causing an estimated $20 billion in economic losses. Though coincidental, the congruity of these events serves as a reminder that the economy and the environment are linked more profoundly than most people think.[1]

Asia's twin economic and ecological crises raise profound questions about the viability of what was until recently viewed as the economic model for developing countries everywhere. One feature of this model is a heavy reliance on infusions of private capital from abroad. The amount of private capital flowing into the "emerging markets" of the developing world exploded in the early 1990s, rising from $44 billion at the beginning of the decade to an all-time high of $244 billion in 1996, according to the World Bank. The inflows of foreign capital fueled a record-breaking economic takeoff in the countries receiving them. China, for instance, which has attracted the greatest volume of funds, expanded its economy at double-digit annual rates in the first half of the 1990s. Several other countries were not far behind. But in the wake of the Asian crisis, the international capital that had been pouring into that region since the beginning of the decade suddenly reversed course as investors raced for the exit. This turnaround brought total private capital flows to emerging markets down to $175 billion in 1997, according to preliminary estimates by the International Monetary Fund (IMF). (See Figure 1.)[2]

Suddenly commentators who just months earlier were extolling the virtues of global economic integration were urgently warning that international financial flows have outgrown existing financial regulatory structures. But few people are paying attention to another critical issue: the extent to which the decade's massive international financial flows to the developing world have undermined the economy's ecological foundations.[3]

Though the booming economies of the developing world raised national incomes, they left ecological devastation in their wake. Urban air pollution levels in many Asian and Latin American cities are among the worst in the world, and natural resources such as forests and fisheries are badly depleted on both continents. Unless action is taken now to reverse current trends, future generations will inherit a biologically impoverished planet and an ecologically unstable world, with uniform tree plantations and vast fish farms inadequately substituting for primary forests and teeming estuaries, and climate change causing catastrophic storms and bigger, more frequent epidemics of infectious diseases.[4]

Understanding the role of private capital flows in all of this is no simple matter, for the environmental implications of this decade's massive movements of money into the developing world, while enormous, are also complex and somewhat contradictory. As investors search the globe for the highest return, they are often drawn to places endowed with bountiful natural resources but handicapped by weak or ineffective environmental laws. Many people and communities are harmed as the environment that sustains them is damaged or destroyed—villagers are displaced by large construction projects, for example, and indigenous peoples watch

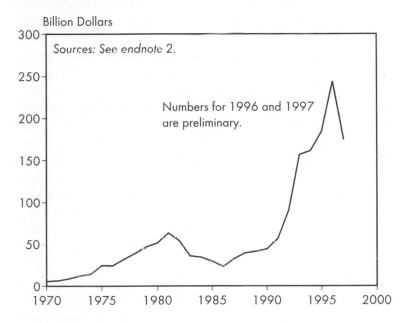

FIGURE 1

International Private Capital Flows to Developing Countries, 1970–97

Billion Dollars

Sources: See endnote 2.

Numbers for 1996 and 1997 are preliminary.

their homelands disappear as timber companies level old-growth forests. Foreign-investment-fed growth also promotes western-style consumerism, pushing car ownership, paper use, and Big Mac consumption rates towards the untenable levels found in the United States—with grave potential consequences for the health of the natural world, the stability of the earth's climate, and the security of food supplies.[5]

But international capital brings environmental benefits as well, most importantly, access to cutting-edge technologies that minimize waste generation and energy use. These new processes can help developing countries leapfrog over the most damaging phases of industrialization, and avoid the kind of costly cleanup bills that many industrial countries are now saddled with.[6]

Policy reforms are needed to steer private capital flows in a more environmentally sound direction. But the levers of change are shifting: the influence wielded by public aid agencies is waning while private sector clout is on the rise. Over the first half of the 1990s, spending on official development assistance fell by more than a quarter in the face of large government budget deficits in donor countries and declining political support for aid. The shrinking public presence coupled with expanding private flows dramatically changed the complexion of North-South development finance. Whereas in 1990 less than half the international capital moving into the developing world came from private sources, by 1996 this share had risen to 86 percent.[7]

This shift in the sources of capital poses a policy challenge, as the private sector is by definition less accountable to the public interest than government agencies are. However, a growing array of "green" international investment strategies are taking shape that aim to shift private capital out of environmentally damaging activities and into enterprises that protect the natural world while profiting from it. Individual investors, private companies, national governments, and international organizations are all central to the success of these efforts. They must be launched quickly and on a large scale if they are to turn around a global economy that pumps 17 million tons of climate-warming carbon from fossil fuel burning into the atmosphere every day, and extinguishes thousands of plant and animal species annually.[8]

The pressure for change is coming from a number of quarters. Around the world, public awareness of the damage that business-as-usual practices inflict on the planet is growing, and grassroots environmental groups are gaining strength. The Asian crisis, meanwhile, has drawn attention to the need to manage global economic integration better. As the process of devising international policies for a globalizing world gets under way in earnest, protecting the natural resource base that underpins the global economy merits a prominent place on the agenda.

Following the Money

The first step in reorienting private capital flows is to track them better, a task made difficult by a paucity of publicly available data. Nonetheless, a rough map can be sketched.

The growth in private flows in the 1990s came on the heels of a number of underlying transformations. For one, many developing countries began welcoming foreign capital with open arms—a dramatic reversal of the practices of earlier decades. They repealed policies that discourage foreign investment, such as ownership restrictions, and promulgated others that encourage it, such as property rights protections. The wave of privatization sweeping the developing world also played a role. Governments in many countries began selling off state-owned monopolies such as electric, gas, and water utilities and telecommunications networks to private bidders, opening up big opportunities for domestic and foreign investors.[9]

Changes in the major industrial countries that supply most of the international capital—mainly Japan, the United States, and West European nations—were important as well. Low interest rates in many of them in the early 1990s prompted investors to look for stronger returns overseas. In addition, some industrial countries loosened controls on their capital markets. This new legal latitude was matched by growing technological power: computerized financial networks allowed investors to shift vast sums of money quickly from one part of the globe to another.[10]

Most of the private funds went to a relatively small group of countries: in the first half of the 1990s, just 12 nations received some three quarters of all of the private inflows. These 12 countries have an enormous impact on the health of the planet by virtue of their relatively large populations, economies, and land masses. (See Table 1 and Figure 2.)[11]

But when foreign capital inflows are measured as a percentage of gross domestic product (GDP) rather than in absolute terms, it becomes clear that foreign capital is also shaping the environmental futures of many smaller coun-

TABLE 1

International Private Capital Flows, Top 12[1]
Developing-Country Recipients, 1996[2]

Country	Total Flows (billion dollars)	Share of GDP[3] (percent)	Amount Per Capita (dollars)
China	52	7	42
Mexico	28	5	294
Brazil	15	3	89
Malaysia	16	14	777
Indonesia	18	6	89
Thailand	13	5	224
Argentina	11	3	323
India	8	1	8
Russia	4	0	25
Turkey	5	1	74
Chile	5	6	317
Hungary	3	18	248

[1] Country ranking is based on cumulative private capital inflows from 1990 to 1995. [2] 1996 numbers for private flows are preliminary. [3] 1995 numbers.

Sources: See endnote 11.

tries as much if not more than those of the big 12. For example, Angola, Papua New Guinea, and Ghana receive higher inflows relative to their size than do Brazil, China, and Mexico—the three largest recipients in absolute terms.[12]

Private capital flows to the developing world take three principal forms: foreign direct investment (FDI) by companies, often through joint ventures with local firms; "portfolio investment" in which stocks and bonds are purchased on local capital markets by individuals and large institutional investors such as insurance companies, mutual funds, and pension plans; and commercial bank loans. (See Table 2.)[13]

Foreign direct investment in developing countries is the largest of these categories, as well as the best documented. It added up to $110 billion in 1996—45 percent of total private flows—and is growing fast, having more than quadrupled since the beginning of the decade. Although investment

TABLE 2

International Private Capital Flows to Developing Countries, 1990 and 1996

Source	1990		1996[1]	
	Amount	Share	Amount	Share
	(billion dollars)	(percent)	(billion dollars)	(percent)
Foreign direct investment	25	56	110	45
Portfolio equity (stocks)	3	7	46	19
Portfolio debt (bonds)	2	5	46	19
Commercial bank loans	3	7	34	14
Other[2]	11	25	8	3
Total	44	100	244	100

[1] Preliminary numbers. [2] Principally export credits from companies and official export credit agencies.

Source: See endnote 13.

from domestic sources is still 10 times as large—$1.2 trillion in 1995—the foreign share has grown rapidly.[14]

FDI has a long and controversial history, dating back at least as far as the eighteenth century, when British and French "East India" companies dominated trading routes between Europe and the "new world." To some critics, FDI is tantamount to colonialism, with the repatriation of profits by multinational corporations robbing host countries of long-term development benefits. But other observers view it more favorably, as both a source of investment capital and a means to acquire technology, know-how, and management skill. Unlike portfolio investors and commercial banks, private companies tend to invest with a long-term time horizon. FDI has the added advantage of not requiring repayment—and thus not contributing to countries' debt burdens.[15]

The quest for natural resources historically has drawn international investors into distant ventures in the developing world. Over the last several decades, however, manufacturing has gradually risen in importance as has, more recent-

FIGURE 2

International Investment Shaping World Environmental Future

TUNISIA
Oil and Gas
Exploration

MEXICO
Toxic Discharges

$28

GUYANA
Mining and
Logging Concessions

EL SALVADOR
Natural Gas
Power Plants

COSTA RICA
Eco-tourism
Bioprospecting

BRAZIL
Logging Concessions

$15

PERU
Gold Mining

**DEMOCRATIC
REPUBLIC OF
CONGO (Zaire)**
Copper Mining
Timber Concessions

CHILE
Bío-Bío River Dams
$5

$11

ARGENTINA
Privatized Water and
Sanitation Services

Top 12 developing country recipients of international private capital flows, based on cumulative inflows from 1990 to 1995. Investment figures are preliminary 1996 numbers (in billions of U.S. dollars). *Sources: See endnote 11.*

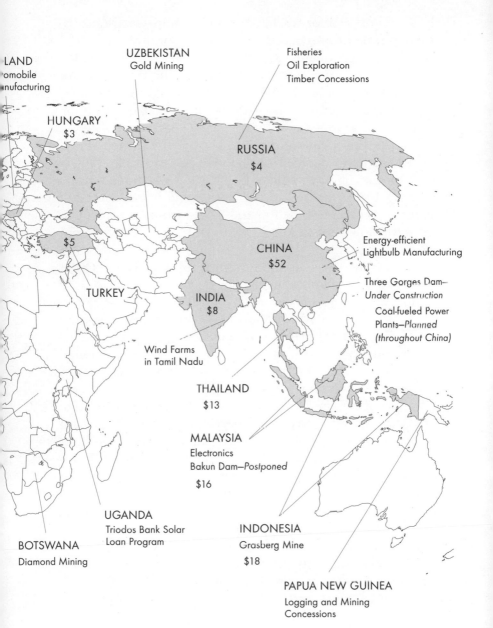

LAND
omobile
nufacturing

UZBEKISTAN
Gold Mining

Fisheries
Oil Exploration
Timber Concessions

HUNGARY
$3

RUSSIA
$4

$5

TURKEY

CHINA
$52

Energy-efficient
Lightbulb Manufacturing

Three Gorges Dam—
Under Construction

Coal-fueled Power
Plants—*Planned*
(throughout China)

INDIA
$8

Wind Farms
in Tamil Nadu

THAILAND
$13

MALAYSIA
Electronics
Bakun Dam—*Postponed*

$16

UGANDA
Triodos Bank Solar
Loan Program

INDONESIA
Grasberg Mine

$18

BOTSWANA
Diamond Mining

PAPUA NEW GUINEA
Logging and Mining
Concessions

ly, the services sector, including construction, electricity dis-tribution, finance, retailing, and telecommunications. The World Bank estimates that the "primary" sector, which includes agriculture, forestry, and mining, now accounts for some 20 percent of all FDI flows to developing countries, while manufacturing makes up less than half of the total, and services more than a third.[16]

Trends in investment outflows from the United States, for which more detailed breakdowns are available, largely confirm these global trends. (See Table 3.) Manufacturing's share of U.S. FDI flows to the developing world decreased slightly over the first half of the 1990s, from 39 percent in 1990 to 36 percent in 1996. Meanwhile, services rose from 22 to 30 percent of the total. Among resource industries, petroleum increased its share from 6 to 14 percent. Other commodities are not tallied as precisely, but appear to have declined as a share of the total over this period.[17]

These broad overall trends mask considerable variation at the country level. The growing predominance of manufac-turing and services is seen most clearly in the big 12 emerging-market countries. For example, manufacturing and services between them account for fully 97 percent of China's incom-ing flows of FDI, and 98 percent of Brazil's accumulated FDI, or "stocks." Yet many other developing countries remain highly dependent on direct natural resource extraction—farm-ing, fishing, logging, mining, and drilling for oil. In Chile, for example, commodities account for nearly 60 percent of FDI stocks, most of it in copper mining. (See Table 4.) Diamond mining attracts most of the FDI that flows to Botswana, while in Tunisia oil and gas development is a big draw. Furthermore, activities such as wood processing and iron smelting are counted as manufacturing, yet they are integrally related to resource extraction and are often found side by side with it.[18]

Companies based in France, Germany, Japan, the United Kingdom, and the United States are the source of most FDI, and between them comprise some 85 percent of the global total. Ranked by the size of their foreign assets, the five largest transnationals as of 1995 were Royal Dutch

TABLE 3

U.S. Foreign Direct Investment Outflows[1]
to Developing Countries, by Sector, 1990 and 1996

Sectors	1990		1996	
	Amount	Share	Amount	Share
	(million dollars)	(percent)	(million dollars)	(percent)
Petroleum	591	6	2,806	14
Manufacturing	3,555	39	7,143	36
Food products	662	7	2,250	11
Chemicals	651	7	2,204	11
Metals	325	4	265	1
Industrial machinery and computer equipment	-7	0	-295	0
Electronic equipment	371	4	881	4
Transportation equipment	605	7	99	0
Other manufacturing[2]	948	10	1,739	9
Services	2,025	22	5,920	30
Wholesale trade	473	5	740	4
Banking	193	2	1,373	7
Finance, insurance and real estate	1,184	13	3,372	17
Other services[3]	175	2	435	2
Other commodities and services[4]	2,992	33	4,074	20
Total	9,163	100	19,943	100

[1] Measures net flows of funds; therefore, some numbers may be negative.
[2] Includes products like tobacco, textiles, paper and newsprint, rubber and plastics.
[3] Includes hotels, advertising, information services and data processing, health, and education. [4] Includes commodities such as agriculture, forestry and mining, and services such as construction, transportation, and public utilities.

Source: See endnote 17.

Shell, Ford, General Electric, Exxon, and General Motors. Their combined foreign assets added up to $339 billion and their overseas work forces numbered some 553,000 people. A significant and increasing share of these totals is in developing countries.[19]

TABLE 4

FDI Stocks,[1] by Sector, Selected Latin American Countries, 1995

Country	Commodities		Manufacturing		Services		Total
	Amount	Share	Amount	Share	Amount	Share	
	(million dollars)	(percent)	(million dollars)	(percent)	(million dollars)	(percent)	(million dollars)
Bolivia[2]	963	76	138	11	169	13	1,270
Brazil[3]	1,144	2	27,301	58	18,584	40	47,029
Chile	8,685	59	2,275	15	3,797	26	14,757
Colombia	7,489	61	2,487	20	2,256	18	12,232
Mexico	935	2	29,967	53	25,163	45	56,065
Peru	1,009	21	655	14	3,161	66	4,825
Venezuela	216	3	3,943	58	2,667	39	6,826

[1] The accumulation of FDI flows over time.   [2] 1994 numbers.   [3] 1993 numbers.

Source: See endnote 18.

Enterprises from several developing and newly industrialized countries have recently become significant sources of capital as well. Companies based in Brazil, Chile, China, Hong Kong, Kuwait, Malaysia, Singapore, South Korea, Taiwan, and Thailand are all investing abroad, often on distant continents. According to estimates by the U.N. Conference on Trade and Development, outflows of direct investment from these countries reached $51 billion in 1996—15 percent of total world outflows.[20]

After FDI, the next most sizable category of private flows to developing countries is "portfolio" investment— accounting for just under 40 percent of the total. This category includes stocks, in which investors own shares in companies, as well as bonds, in which private investors make long-term loans to governments or businesses at fixed interest rates. Over the past decade, stock markets have been established in many unlikely corners of the globe, including China, Russia, and Uganda. At the same time, the amount of funds flowing into these markets has soared. Around the world, the number of funds specifically devoted to emerging markets has climbed steeply in recent years—from just 28 in 1986 to over 1,000 in 1995. Their combined assets jumped from under $2 billion in 1986 to $132 billion a decade later. Popular sectors for investment include finance, infrastructure, manufacturing, mining, telecommunications, transportation, and utilities. Despite its apparent novelty, overseas portfolio investing is not without historical precedent: bonds purchased by British investors helped finance the construction of railroads in Argentina, Brazil, and the United States during the nineteenth century.[21]

Portfolio investments are the most volatile ingredient in the mix of private flows. Investors may withdraw their funds quickly if they lose confidence in a country's economic prospects, often setting in motion a ripple effect in other emerging markets. This happened in 1994 during Mexico's peso crisis. Portfolio equity (stock) investments had jumped from just $3 billion in 1990 to $45 billion in 1993. The Mexican crisis triggered a sharp decline worldwide over the next two years, although by 1996 portfolio equity investments had bounced back, reaching an all-time annual high of $46 billion, or 19 percent of total private flows. Bond issues largely mirrored the portfolio equity trend. They increased from $2 billion in 1990 to $36 billion in 1993. After a two-year decline, they climbed to the new height of $46 billion in 1996. Now it is Asia's turn for a rollercoaster ride. The ongoing economic crisis there has led to a sharp fall-off in portfolio investment, although so far it does not appear to be triggering a loss of confidence in other emerging markets. It remains to be seen how quickly the Asian region will recover from its current troubles.[22]

Commercial bank lending is the other major category of private capital flowing into the developing world—it accounted for 14 percent of total private flows in 1996, or $34 billion. Commercial loans had climbed to this level from just $3 billion at the beginning of the decade. But the increase may have been short-lived: early estimates indicate that commercial loans declined substantially in volume in 1997 as a result of Asia's troubles.[23]

International commercial bank lending also has a long history. During the eighteenth century, for example, "Dutch capital was to be found in every large commercial venture of Europe and was lent to governments far and wide," according to historians R.R. Palmer and Joel Colton. More recently, commercial bank loans began to flow rapidly into the developing world during the 1970s, when the "petrodollars" piling up in northern banks as a result of high oil prices made them desperate to find new borrowers. Rising interest rates and questionable investment decisions placed a staggering debt burden on recipient countries, paving the way for the debt crisis of the 1980s and the consequent stagnation in lending.[24]

In the resurgence of lending in the mid-1990s, the recipients were more likely to be private enterprises than governments. Much of the money came in the form of short-term loans to national banks, which they in turn lent to local borrowers for a range of purposes, including questionable real estate investments such as those now coming unraveled in Asia, as well as construction projects such as highways and power plants.[25]

Natural Wealth—
to Squander or Husband?

International investment in resource extraction is now flowing rapidly into many countries that are richly endowed with natural assets such as primary forests, mineral and petroleum reserves, and biological diversity. Investors are being drawn to these countries by rich natural resource bases, as well as by a movement in many of them to privatize natural resource industries and loosen restrictions on foreign ownership.[26]

Countries rich in natural wealth all too often squander this bounty by investing in ill-conceived projects that mine natural resources for the short-term economic gain of political elites, at the expense of local peoples and future generations. A wiser long-term strategy would be to funnel capital into economic activities that preserve natural endowments, as a number of innovative experiments now under way aim to do.

The growing flow of funds into natural resource extraction in developing countries is particularly pronounced within the mining industry. From 1991 to 1997, international spending on exploration for nonferrous metals grew six times in Latin America, almost quadrupled in the Pacific region, and doubled in Africa, while leveling off in the traditional mining countries of Canada and the United States. (See Table 5.) Spending on exploration for gold has been growing particularly fast, accounting for nearly two thirds of total spending on metals exploration in recent years. In what *Business Week* calls a "great global gold rush," prospectors are increasingly shifting from their traditional locales in Canada, South Africa, and the United States in search of gold mines abroad.[27]

The U.S. mining industry blames environmentalists for the migration, arguing that tighter environmental regulations have made domestic mining a difficult and expensive proposition. More to the point is the fact that host countries are inviting international investors in with open arms; some 70 countries have rewritten their national mining codes in recent years with the aim of encouraging investment. Yet few are devoting similar energy to strengthening environmental laws and enforcement. And mining takes a heavy environmental toll: for every kilogram of gold produced in the United States, some 3 million kilograms of waste rock are left behind. Prime mining sites are often located in previously undisturbed forests or wilderness areas. Besides disturbing valuable ecosystems, this activity also disrupts the lives of the indigenous peoples who inhabit them: an estimated 50 percent of gold produced in the next 20 years will come from indigenous peoples' lands. Toxic by-products of mining can poison the rivers that local people drink from, and the mining operations themselves often destroy the forests and fields that they rely on for sustenance.[28]

Like mining companies, multinational oil and gas firms are continually scouring the globe looking for new development opportunities, as the most accessible fields in industrial countries have already been tapped. More than 90 percent of known oil and gas reserves are now in the developing world. The major oil and gas companies are thus increasingly striking deals—and oil—in the Central Asian republics, deep in the South American rainforest, and off Asian and West African shores. As with mineral extraction, the environmental and social costs are high when previously remote and pristine areas are opened up to development.[29]

Logging by international companies poses yet another threat to the world's rapidly dwindling tropical forests and the indigenous peoples and diverse plant and animal life harbored in them. For many years now, companies from countries with depleted forests have been turning their chainsaws loose overseas. European firms, for instance, have long been active in Africa: in the early 1980s, some 90 percent of log-

TABLE 5

Worldwide Metals[1] Exploration Spending,[2] by Location, 1991 and 1997

Region	1991		1997	
	Amount	Share	Amount	Share
	(million dollars)	(percent)	(million dollars)	(percent)
Canada	430	23	436	11
Australia	353	19	673	17
United States	341	18	365	9
Africa	315	17	663	16
Latin America	200	11	1,170	29
Pacific region	125	7	440	11
Rest of the world[3]	82	4	283	7
Total	1,846	100[4]	4,030	100

[1] Includes precious, base, and other non-ferrous hard-rock metals. [2] Based on the budgets of major mining companies that represent 80 percent of worldwide exploration spending. [3] Includes Europe, Former Soviet Union, Middle East and Asia (excluding Pacific nations). [4] Columns may not add up to 100 percent due to rounding.

Sources: See endnote 27.

ging operations in Gabon were foreign-owned, as were some 77 percent of those in Congo, nearly 90 percent of those in Cameroon, and virtually all of those in Liberia. At least 17 European companies were operating in Côte d'Ivoire alone in 1990, and they have shown no sign of letting up in recent years. Japanese firms, for their part, joined forces with local companies in the 1970s and 1980s to decimate the forests of Southeast Asian countries such as Indonesia and Malaysia.[30]

With their own forests greatly reduced, logging companies from Indonesia, Malaysia, and elsewhere in Asia are now themselves investing overseas. Asian companies are vying for vast timber concessions in Africa, Asia, and Latin America that threaten some of the world's last remaining untouched forests. Brazil, Cambodia, Congo, the Democratic Republic of Congo (formerly Zaire), Guyana, Nicaragua, Papua New Guinea, the Solomon Islands, and Suriname are among the countries that have given or are on the brink of giving away the rights to log large tracts of primary forests—often at prices that do not reflect their marketplace value let alone their ecological worth. Some of the companies involved have a long history of catastrophic environmental destruction, tax evasion, and corruption—a fact that does not augur well for their new hosts.[31]

International companies are also stepping up their investments in related wood-products industries such as sawmills and pulp and paper operations that feed off of steady streams of locally supplied wood. Some 15 U.S. wood-products companies have set up shop in Mexico since the North American Free Trade Agreement (NAFTA) was ratified in 1994. And in Brazil and Chile, international companies have joined forces with local investors to build pulp and paper mills supplied by vast monoculture tree plantations that are sprouting up at a rapid rate.[32]

Large amounts of international capital also flow into cash crops, such as bananas, coffee, cotton, soybeans, and tobacco. The expansion of export-oriented production often requires the clearing of primary forests or the appropriation of land once devoted to subsistence agriculture. Plans to increase soybean production in the Amazon basin are necessitating the construction of an extensive network of canals, highways, and railroads in order to get the crop to market. Although the soybeans themselves are being grown principally by domestic farmers for export to Asia and Europe, international capital is invested in their processing as well as in the construction of the associated infrastructure. In another ongoing controversy, a planned investment by a Kansas-based company in a sugar cane plantation in Argentina threatens to destroy large swaths of forest—and with it the habitat of rare species such as jaguar and toucan as well as the semi-nomadic way of life of the local Kolla people. [33]

Forests are not the only ecosystem coming under growing assault: the world's oceans are also vulnerable to the spread of the global economy. With many northern waters already overfished, the world's large factory fishing fleets are heading south in search of fish to please northern palates.

For example, access agreements have allowed fleets from Europe, Russia, South Korea, Japan, and Taiwan to ply African waters. The countries involved granted this access at cut rates. Meanwhile, local subsistence fishers are increasingly hauling up empty nets.[34]

Today's boom in natural resource extraction is being driven in no small measure by a cold reality of today's global economy: many developing countries are starved for cash. Commercial bank loans in the 1970s left many of them weighed down by large debt burdens. Desperate for foreign exchange with which to repay these loans, countries have sometimes been forced to sell off the "family silver." The amount of money at stake is substantial: the heavily indebted government of Senegal, for instance, takes in a sizable share of its revenue from payments made by vessels from Asia, Canada, and Europe in exchange for access to the country's fisheries. Similarly, a package of timber concessions under consideration in Suriname in 1995 would have earned $500 million for the government—an amount roughly equal to the country's GDP. Publicity about the environmental damage that would result from the proposed deals has prevented them from going forward, although rumors abound that other concession agreements are on the table.[35]

Though natural resource extraction has generated foreign exchange and government revenue, it has often failed to translate into long-term economic success for resource-dependent countries. Research by Jeffrey Sachs and Andrew Warner of Harvard University demonstrates that countries rich in natural resources have on average performed worse economically than resource-poor countries in recent decades. A range of factors lie behind this counterintuitive result, including the volatility of commodity prices as well as the tendency for resource extraction to be poorly linked to the rest of the economy. In addition, governments have often failed to negotiate favorable financial terms in concession contracts, which has led to taking in less revenue than they could have. And those revenues that have been generated have not always been well spent. Rather than financing educational and health care systems, they have too often been used to line the pockets of corrupt officials or to further enrich local elites.[36]

Another limitation of resource extraction is that it is a one-shot deal. Once a country's minerals and oil have been extracted and its forests cleared, its options for the future will be greatly diminished. A better strategy is to harvest the bounty of natural wealth in a way that leaves natural capital intact for future generations.

"Bioprospecting" is one example of this approach. Drug and seed companies have long used the genetic diversity of the developing world to create new products. Yet even when a traditional crop variety proves essential for breeding a new line of seeds, or when a wild plant yields some valuable new drug, corporations have rarely paid anything for access to the genetic resource. The Convention on Biological Diversity signed at the Earth Summit in 1992 gives nations the right to charge for access to genetic resources, and it allows them to pass national legislation setting the terms of any bioprospecting agreements. The intent of the treaty is to provide a strong conservation incentive by encouraging countries to view genetic diversity as a source of potential profits. And the growing power of biotechnology, which allows for much more direct manipulation of genes than was previously possible, suggests that the profit potential will continue to rise in the years ahead.[37]

A year before the Earth Summit, Merck and Company, the world's largest pharmaceuticals firm, and Costa Rica's Instituto Nacional de Biodiversidad (INBio) reached a precedent-setting bioprospecting agreement roughly along the lines of those envisioned by the treaty. Merck agreed to pay INBio $1.35 million in support of conservation programs in exchange for access to the country's plants, microbes, and insects, as well as royalty payments when any discovery makes its way into a product. Though widely hailed as an important step forward, the agreement has also generated its share of controversy. Critics of the agreement question whether or not the royalty rate was set at a fair level, and to what extent the economic benefits will reach the local peoples whose knowledge of medicinal properties is so central to making the deal work.[38]

A number of other bioprospecting programs are now taking shape—some of which offer better models for the distribution of revenues. A bioprospecting initiative in Suriname, for instance, involves a number of different partners, including indigenous healers, a Surinamese pharmaceutical company, the U.S.-based Bristol Myers Squibb company, the environmental group Conservation International, and the Missouri Botanical Gardens. Royalties from any drugs developed will be channeled into a range of local institutions, including non-governmental organizations (NGOs), the national pharmaceutical company, and the forest service. In addition, a Forest Peoples Fund has been established to support small-scale development projects that benefit local indigenous peoples.[39]

Ecotourism is another possible vehicle for channeling international investment capital into the preservation of threatened ecosystems, if it is pursued in an ecologically sensitive manner. Costa Rica is leading the way. The country's moist cloud forests, sandy beaches, and dry deciduous forests have made tourism the top foreign exchange earner, surpassing traditional export mainstays such as bananas and coffee. Since ecotourism is not generally capital-intensive, domestic investment may often be sufficient for underwriting much of the industry. But even ecotourism has its infrastructure: international investment may find a role in upgrading airports and building the kind of carefully conceived, small-scale, low-impact hotels that are consistent with the industry's conservation goals.[40]

Finally, the last few years have seen a flurry of activity aimed at generating consumer pressure for sustainably harvested commodities through certification and eco-labeling programs. The pioneer in these efforts is the Forest Stewardship Council (FSC), an independent body established in 1993 to set standards for sustainable forest production through a cooperative process involving timber traders and retailers as well as environmental organizations and forest dwellers. Although certified timber accounts for only a miniscule share of the wood traded internationally today, demand is growing fast, and has more than doubled since 1994. A few international investors are setting themselves up to tap into this expanding market. Precious Woods Management Ltd., for one, a Swiss-owned firm, has established a subsidiary in the Brazilian Amazon that is now harvesting timber from an operation certified as well managed by SmartWood, a certification program sponsored by the New York-based Rainforest Alliance and accredited by the FSC.[41]

Similar efforts are under way for other commodities. Rainforest Alliance has also helped to create a certification and labeling program for banana companies. To be certified as an "ECO-OK" banana producer, plantations must agree, among other criteria, not to clear any virgin forests and to monitor rivers and wells for pesticide residues. In a major victory, Chiquita Brands has already signed up 29 plantations and has pledged to certify all of its Latin American operations by 2000. In another comparable effort, the United Kingdom branch of the World Wildlife Fund has teamed up with one of the world's largest seafood product-manufacturers, Anglo-Dutch Unilever, to spearhead the creation of a Marine Stewardship Council along the lines of the FSC to devise criteria for sustainable fish harvesting.[42]

The Global Factory

The spectacular growth of East Asian countries in the past decade has come despite—and perhaps even because of—a marked shortage of natural resources. Instead, the economic takeoff in these countries resulted from rapid growth in manufacturing—much of it destined for export markets and financed by large infusions of foreign capital. Many countries around the world are now trying to replicate this strategy. Yet from an environmental point of view, the manufacturing takeoff is a two-edged sword: international investment in manufacturing sometimes helps developing countries adopt new technologies that produce less waste and use fewer raw materials than standard machinery; yet it can also bring highly polluting industries that jeopardize human and ecological health.[43]

The category of manufacturing covers a vast array of products and processes. It includes relatively low-tech yet labor-intensive enterprises such as textile production and food processing, as well as high-tech industries such as chemicals, electronics, and pharmaceuticals. Although it is difficult to generalize, labor-intensive activities tend to be less environmentally damaging than capital-intensive ones because, by definition, they use less energy and materials and tend to produce fewer damaging by-products. Capital-intensive industries such as chemicals, in contrast, are often highly polluting.[44]

From an environmental point of view, the manufacturing takeoff is a two-edged sword.

In part because of the low cost of their labor, developing countries moved first into the lower-tech industries as they diversified their economies. Their share of world production of textiles, for instance, increased from 23 to 39 percent between 1975 and 1996, while their share of iron and steel smelting rose from 12 to 36 percent. In recent years, however, many developing countries have also moved into high-tech activities, such as chemicals, electronics, and pharmaceuticals—industries that carry substantial environmental risks. Their share of world production of industrial chemicals increased from 17 percent in 1990 to 25 percent in 1996, and that of electrical machinery rose from 13 to 20 percent over this period.[45]

Foreign direct investments largely mirror these broader changes, with the World Bank reporting in 1997 that high-tech industries such as chemicals and electronics were accounting for a growing share of FDI manufacturing flows to the developing world. For example, the chemical industry's share of total U.S. manufacturing FDI in developing countries increased from 18 percent in 1990 to 31 percent in 1996, and electronics equipment climbed from 10 to 12 percent of the total over this period. Almost 45 percent of U.S. capital flows to Argentina in 1996 were for chemicals, and in Malaysia that year more than half of U.S. funds went into electronics.[46]

Studies suggest that industries are generally drawn to locations by the cost and quality of labor, the availability of natural resources, or the access to large markets. In most cases, environmental control costs alone are not high enough to be a determining factor in location decisions. But even if companies move to the developing world for other reasons, they may take advantage of lax environmental laws and enforcement once there.[47]

The current surge of international investment in manufacturing thus brings with it environmental dangers. Hazardous industries, such as battery manufacturers, chemical companies, and computer manufacturing and assembly facilities, are becoming increasingly concentrated in countries where safety practices and environmental enforcement and monitoring are rudimentary at best. A recent review of 22 computer-related companies based in industrial countries by the San Jose, California-based Silicon Valley Toxics Coalition found that more than half of their collective manufacturing and assembly operations—processes intensive in their use of acids, solvents, and toxic gases—are now located in developing countries.[48]

In a few instances, moreover, relaxed environmental enforcement does appear to have been a motivating factor in companies' location decisions. The debate over the 1993 North American Free Trade Agreement put the spotlight on one notoriously polluted region where this seems to have been the case for some firms—the border between northern Mexico and the United States. That area is the site of nearly 2,000 mostly foreign-owned manufacturing plants known as maquiladoras. In the city of Mexicali, near the California border, more than a quarter of the factory operators surveyed in the late 1980s said that Mexico's lax environmental enforcement influenced their decision to locate there. These and other companies helped make the area an environmental disaster zone: a 1991 survey conducted by the U.S.

National Toxics Campaign found toxic discharges at three quarters of the maquiladoras sampled. Chemicals known to cause cancer, birth defects, and brain damage were being emptied into open ditches that ran through the shantytowns around the factories.[49]

The maquiladoras region is but one of some 230 export or special processing zones that span 70 countries and collectively employ some 44 million workers. These zones normally permit goods to be imported duty free, on the condition that they then be used to produce exported products. A range of other inducements may be used to encourage companies to locate production in these zones. There is considerable evidence that one lure is often a casual attitude toward substandard labor practices such as dangerous working conditions and restrictions on the right to organize. Although no comprehensive data on the question have been gathered, it is likely that environmental abuses are equally common. In the coastal Cavite province near Manila, for instance, local fishers accuse Taiwanese, Korean, and other factories in special economic zones adjacent to Manila Bay of dumping pollutants that are responsible for killing off thousands of fish. And the Chinese National Environmental Protection Agency has accused firms from these same countries of setting up shop in China in order to flee tougher environmental regulations at home.[50]

Hazardous industries are increasingly concentrated in countries where safety practices are rudimentary.

Beyond spreading hazardous manufacturing processes, international investment also spurs demand in the developing world for products that typify the wasteful consumer societies of the North. The worldwide spread of fast food companies is a case in point. McDonald's, for instance—which promotes consumption of grain- and water-intensive beef—is moving rapidly into South Africa, which it sees as a springboard for the continent as a whole. As the managing director of McDonald's South Africa puts it: "We want to develop a Big Mac culture throughout sub-Saharan Africa."[51]

The major multinational automobile companies are also expanding into the "emerging markets" of Asia, Eastern Europe, and Latin America. If current projections hold, some three quarters of the auto factories to be built over the next three years will go up in these countries. European, Japanese, U.S., and South Korean companies are competing aggressively to build the plants. General Motors recently sank some $2.2 billion into a "four-plant strategy" to build nearly identical facilities simultaneously in Argentina, China, Poland, and Thailand. And nine of the world's major automakers—including Daewoo Motor, Fiat, General Motors, and Mercedes-Benz—have moved into India in just the last few years. If these countries develop auto-centric transportation systems along the lines of the U.S. model, there will be grave consequences for local air pollution and food security, not to mention global climate change.[52]

A better route would be for developing countries to learn from the mistakes of the industrial world, and move directly to the technologies of tomorrow—which will be far cleaner and more efficient in their use of energy and raw materials than the equipment typically in use today. International investment can help expedite this transition: a 1992 World Bank study compared the rates at which 60 countries were adopting a cleaner wood pulping process, and concluded that countries open to foreign investment acquired the new technology far more rapidly than those that were closed to it. Limited evidence suggests that the recent move to privatize state-owned factories by selling them to domestic or foreign private investors sometimes promotes cleaner industrial processes. One reason is that privatization eliminates the conflict of interest that arises when the government is both producer and regulator. In addition, the pressure to turn a profit introduces an incentive to adopt manufacturing techniques that reduce energy and materials use and thus diminish pollution.[53]

Already, a number of new, more environmentally sound products are being produced in developing countries through joint ventures with international firms. Compact fluorescent light bulbs, for example, first produced in the United States, are increasingly manufactured in the developing world. In 1995, China made 80–100 million of these energy-efficient bulbs—more than any other country. The funding and technology came in part through joint ventures with lighting firms based in Hong Kong, Japan, the Netherlands, and Taiwan. Compact fluorescents produced by joint ventures consistently outrank those of domestic companies in meeting performance standards such as efficiency and durability. Renewable energy components are also now being made in developing countries. India, for instance, has become a major manufacturer of advanced wind turbines with the help of technology obtained through joint ventures and licensing agreements with Danish, Dutch, and German firms. It has become the world's fourth largest wind power producer, with an installed capacity of more than 800 megawatts.[51]

The Infrastructure Boom

People in developing countries lack access to many services crucial to a high quality of life. About 1.2 billion people—more than one fifth of humanity—have no access to clean drinking water, some 2 billion have no electricity, and nearly 3 billion lack adequate sanitation services. Meeting these needs is an important goal of developing-country governments. But building infrastructure for electricity, transportation, and sewage treatment often involves large construction projects that strain national treasuries and the natural world. The challenge is to provide these services in ways that are affordable, environmentally sound, and socially equitable.[55]

Against this backdrop, one of the most dramatic trends of the 1990s has been the rapid rate at which developing-country governments have turned many traditionally public infrastructure activities over to the private sector. Private companies are now building power plants, telecommunications networks, water treatment plants, dams, and toll roads in many corners of the globe, and two thirds of the finance comes from investors abroad. Inflows of foreign funds for infrastructure construction climbed from $2.6 billion at the beginning of the 1990s to an estimated $22.3 billion by 1995. Seventy percent of this money went to private companies rather than governments, which have traditionally owned and managed most large infrastructure projects. Over this period, power projects accounted for 44 percent of the total, telecommunications for 30 percent, transport for 13 percent, and other types of projects for the remaining 13 percent.[56]

The privatization of services that have normally been within the public domain raises complicated and controversial questions of accountability, equity, and environmental sustainability. When it is done right, the burst of private infrastructure building can have the benefit of providing hundreds of millions of people with much-needed services that are beyond the financial reach of cash-starved governments. When it is done wrong, privatization leaves environmental degradation and social disruption in its wake.

The projected price tags are indeed staggering. According to the Asian Development Bank, Asia alone needs infrastructure investment of some $10 trillion over the next 30 years, mainly in the power, transport, and telecommunications sectors. Yet these numbers are inflated by an emphasis on supply-side solutions: the construction of new infrastructure ought not to take precedence over more cost-effective strategies on the demand side, such as plugging leaky pipes to save water or caulking windows to cut down on energy use.[57]

The numerous power sector projects now in the pipeline have particularly serious implications for the environment—especially for the quality of the air and the stability of the climate. Over the next several decades, the bulk of new global investment in the power sector is projected to take place in developing countries. The world's ability to avert a catastrophic warming of the atmosphere will depend in no small measure on what kind of power plants are built.[58]

A sizable share of current international investment in the power sector is bankrolling multimillion-dollar coal- and oil-fired power plants that produce prodigious amounts of both local air pollutants and greenhouse gases.

For instance, international investors are queuing up to participate in the construction of the more than 500 mid-sized power plants that China plans to construct by 2010—equivalent to more than double China's current generating capacity. Many of these will be fueled by coal. This will add to the country's already overwhelming burden of air-pollution-related disease and death. And current emissions trends suggest that China, now the world's second largest emitter of carbon, could well surpass the United States and top the list by 2010. Many other countries are heading

Privatization of traditionally public services raises questions of accountability, equity, and environmental sustainability.

down the same path. In Indonesia, for example, $1.82 billion in private bank loans helped build the immense 1,230 megawatt coal-fired "Paiton I" power project.[59]

More promising are the plans of many countries to build cleaner, gas-fired plants, often using advanced gas turbines and cogeneration (the combined production of heat and electricity in factories and buildings). Brazil, El Salvador, India, Indonesia, Mexico, and Vietnam are among the countries where foreign-funded gas-fired plants are either under construction or being planned. Yet gas development has its own environmental liabilities, including the construction of massive pipelines to transport the gas from remote areas. These pipeline projects are generally paralleled by service roads, which open up previously remote areas to settlement and other incursions. "Welcome to the 1990s version of Rudyard Kipling's Great Game," notes the *Wall Street Journal*. "Instead of imperial powers scrambling for territory in Central Asia, giant energy companies, mainly U.S. ones, are vying to dominate access routes between Latin America's natural-gas fields and its big cities." Similar rushes are under way in Central and Southeast Asia and in the Middle East.[60]

The private sector is also stepping in to supply equipment and finance for large hydro dams that provide electricity, water for irrigation, and flood control—though often at enormous environmental and social cost. In China, international companies are competing fiercely for contracts to help build the Three Gorges Dam on the Yangtze River, which is projected to supply roughly a tenth of China's electricity when completed around 2009. The dam is expected to flood 60,730 hectares of land and 160 towns, forcing the resettlement of some 1.3 million people. The Chinese government has announced that it will finance the dam through commercial bank loans, bond offerings, and stock investments. Environmental groups are publicizing the role of international financiers in these transactions. In early 1997, a number of U.S. financial institutions including Lehman Brothers and Morgan Stanley underwrote $330 million in bonds issued by China's State Development Bank—the principal financier of the Three Gorges project. The same year, environmental activists successfully pressured a Japanese investment house to cancel a similar offering by revealing that the funds would support the construction of Three Gorges.[61]

These activists can take some hope from the fact that another controversial dam project has been halted for the time being, having failed to pass the market test. The proposed 2,400-megawatt Bakun hydroelectric project on Sarawak, the Malaysian portion of the island of Borneo, would require clearing 69,000 hectares of rainforest, flooding an area the size of Singapore, and displacing 9,500 indigenous people. Efforts to sell shares to international investors in the controversial project on the Kuala Lumpur stock exchange have so far met with little success, forcing one of the project's financial backers to cancel a planned stock issuance. Then, in the wake of Malaysia's financial troubles, the Prime Minister announced in September 1997 that the project has been put on hold indefinitely—although the government says that it plans to proceed with rechanneling the river and relocating some villagers.[62]

Other investors aim to funnel money into smaller-scale,

less-centralized approaches to meeting the energy needs of the developing world. The Triodos Bank, for one, a Dutch investment bank, launched a Solar Investment Fund in late 1996 whose purpose is to finance loans in Africa, Asia, and Latin America for household solar electric systems in rural communities lacking access to grid-supplied power. Two Washington, D.C.-based enterprises have similar plans: the Solar Electric Light Company raised $2.5 million in private backing in 1997 from Swiss, German, and U.S. investors for operations in China, India, Sri Lanka, Vietnam, and elsewhere, and SunLight Power International has received some $4.75 million from a German venture capital fund and a Swiss insurance company. It plans to provide off-grid photovoltaic-generated electricity to communities in Africa, Asia, and Latin America. On a somewhat larger scale, Amoco and Enron are looking for finance for a joint venture to build a 50-megawatt photovoltaic power plant in India.[63]

The takeoff in telecommunications investments also holds promise as one element in a broader leapfrogging strategy for developing countries. Many of these nations are poised to skip over the cable-based stage of telecommunications development and go straight to the wireless era of cellular and satellite-based technology. This leap would enable people living in remote locations to plug into the information highway, without either the economic or the environmental costs involved in stringing copper wires for hundreds of thousands of kilometers through remote regions. The implications for development are profound: "I have met people in Morocco who are doing desktop publishing for firms in Paris," reports World Bank President James Wolfensohn. "Ghanaian traders are using cellular phones to get their cocoa quotes; and in Brazil Amazon chiefs are using video cameras and satellites to communicate with each other."[64]

Another rapid growth area for international private infrastructure investment is the provision of water and sanitation services. With investment needs in the water and sanitation area in the developing world adding up to at least $600 billion over the next decade, according to World Bank estimates, governments clearly need private help. Over the last few years, a handful of British and French companies have moved aggressively into this market. For example, the French company Lyonnaise des Eaux entered into a concession agreement in 1993 with several partners to invest more than $4 billion in upgrading and expanding water and sanitation services in Buenos Aires. It has also joined forces with Compagnie Générale des Eaux and other partners to provide similar services in Mexico City.[65]

Like all other aspects of privatization, granting concessions for water and waste treatment services to private investors is controversial. Critics worry that the profit motive will provide little incentive to protect the ecological integrity of watersheds or to expand coverage to the poor. Furthermore, companies whose bottom line depends on selling as much water as possible have little incentive to invest in water conservation programs. Yet proponents argue that governments retain full powers to set the terms of private concession contracts. For instance, the Buenos Aires water concession contract stipulates what share of the population is to be provided with potable water and sewerage services, and by what date. Mexico City's wastewater treatment concession contract lays down minimum effluent standards and provides for penalties in the event that they are not met.[66]

Given the lack of effective environmental enforcement in much of the developing world, there is ample reason to question whether or not the companies will be held to their word. Yet in the case of Buenos Aires, at least, the experiment so far seems to have been mainly a success. Within the first two years, 400,000 new water and 250,000 new sewerage connections were made, many in low-income neighborhoods. The quality of drinking water also improved and the city's customary summer water shortages became a thing of the past. Furthermore, water and sewage rates declined by 17 percent after the concession contract went into effect. This was less than the 27 percent cut stipulated in the initial concession agreement, but a substantial drop nonetheless.[67]

Providers of waste management and other environmental clean-up services are also vying to enter emerging markets. Demand for pollution control and pollution prevention technologies is growing at double-digit rates in many parts of Asia, Eastern Europe, and Latin America as these countries begin to face up to the magnitude of their clean-up challenges. In India, for instance, a U.S. Department of Commerce study projects that demand for environmental technologies will climb by 25 percent per year through the end of the decade, with energy and transportation ventures, solid waste management, and recycling enterprises high on the list of needs. A recent U.S. and Canadian environment trade mission to the country attracted nearly 300 companies seeking joint ventures and other forms of collaboration.[68]

Demand for pollution control and pollution prevention technologies is growing at double-digit rates.

The Power of the Purse

The rapid infusion of private capital into emerging markets has led to confusion on the part of those accustomed to the more familiar world of aid-financed development. Somewhat nostalgically, a report by Friends of the Earth notes that "with yesterday's centralized funding, NGOs could lobby particular organizations and stage demonstrations outside meetings. But it is difficult to effectively influence something as nebulous as private capital flows." Though difficult, it is by no means impossible. A number of leverage points offer promise for shaping the developing world's environmental future, most notably the power wielded by public and private investors themselves.[69]

Multilateral and bilateral aid and export credit agencies remain critical players, although sometimes in new roles.

Attaching environmental conditions to the programs of these agencies that support private investments is an effective way of using a limited amount of aid money as an environmental screen to influence far larger pools of private capital.

Perhaps the biggest opportunity involves the World Bank and two affiliated agencies, the International Finance Corporation (IFC) and the Multilateral Investment Guarantee Agency (MIGA). Though the World Bank has traditionally made loans only to governments, in the last few years it has begun to use some of its funds to back commercial lending to the private sector. IFC, which lends directly to private enterprises, is much smaller than the Bank itself. But on average each dollar IFC lends is attached to five dollars of private investment—a ratio that greatly expands this agency's influence. MIGA also promotes private investment, principally by insuring against political risks, such as expropriation, civil disturbance, and breach of contract. Since it issued its first contract in 1990, MIGA has guaranteed nearly 300 contracts involving almost $20 billion of foreign direct investment. The World Bank estimates that at least 10 percent of all private sector investment in the developing world is now covered by at least one of these types of support, and this number is expected to increase steadily in the years ahead.[70]

Both IFC and MIGA are involved in many large investment projects with heavy ecological impacts. More than half of IFC's outstanding portfolio of $18.9 billion in 1997 was invested in environmentally sensitive sectors such as automobile manufacturing, chemicals, construction, infrastructure, and mining. In recent years, IFC has helped finance a chemical factory in Mexico, a gold mine in Zimbabwe, and a coal-fired power plant in the Philippines, to cite just a few examples.[71]

After a decade of pressure from non-governmental organizations and determined efforts by committed insiders, the World Bank now has an extensive set of environmental and social policies, which cover issues such as environmental impact assessments of projects and protection of wilderness areas and the rights of indigenous peoples. In theory, all

Bank agencies including IFC and MIGA are bound by these policies. Yet Bank officials acknowledge that actual operating procedures have sometimes been different in private sector operations, in part due to confidentiality concerns. And, by its own admission, the Bank itself—let alone IFC and MIGA —does not always follow its own rules.[72]

Since taking office in 1995, Bank President James Wolfensohn has pledged to step up environmental enforce-ment in all branches of the institution, including those that involve the private sector. More specifically, he has pledged to work with the Bank's board to clarify exactly how World Bank policies apply to private sector operations, a process that is now under way. Efforts are also afoot to give these policies teeth by expanding the scope of the organization's indepen-dent inspection panel to cover private sector projects.[73]

Although these would be important steps forward, there are nonetheless substantial limits to the Bank's power over the private sector. These limits were brought home by a recent case involving an IFC loan to a privately owned Chilean electric utility for the construction of a series of dams on the scenic Bío-Bío River, an area that is home to 8,000 indigenous people and to myriad rare plant and animal species. IFC commissioned an independent review of the project that concluded the utility had repeatedly violated the environmental and social conditions written into the loan agreement. But in the face of Wolfensohn's protests, the util-ity simply prepaid its IFC loan, thereby releasing itself from any of the environmental strings attached to the money.[74]

Bilateral export promotion agencies offer another prong of attack. Like IFC and MIGA, these agencies support many large projects with large environmental impacts. The U.S. Overseas Private Investment Corporation (OPIC), for instance, provides political risk insurance similar to that offered by MIGA. The agency has underwritten numerous environmentally damaging activities, including mining in Indonesia and Peru; fishing, logging, and mining in Siberia; and the construction of coal-fired power plants in Indonesia, the Philippines, Thailand, and Morocco.[75]

OPIC has had an environmental policy in place since the late seventies that has been gradually strengthened in the years since. It now requires adherence to World Bank environmental guidelines for all projects, and also to U.S. standards for some of them, including mining projects. In 1995, environmentalists successfully lobbied the agency to enforce this policy by canceling the $100 million in political risk insurance it was providing to the Indonesian operations of a New Orleans-based mining company, Freeport McMoran Copper and Gold. The policy covered the company's operations at the Grasberg Mine in the Indonesian province of Irian Jaya, on the island of New Guinea. This mine is one of the world's largest, with copper, gold, and silver deposits reportedly worth more than $60 billion at 1996 market prices. The mine was dumping 100,000 tons of tailings into nearby rivers every day, which local people said was contaminating the fish they ate and the water they drank. The clogged rivers were also flooding large swaths of rainforest and threatening a diverse array of forest species.[76]

As with Bío-Bío, however, later developments in the Freeport case show how difficult it can be to make a victory stick. A year after its initial decision, OPIC reinstated Freeport's policy after the company agreed to establish a $100 million trust fund to clean up the site at the end of the mine's life. Then just a few months later, Freeport decided it could do without OPIC's help and canceled its policy.[77]

At the urging of environmental groups, U.S. President Bill Clinton announced plans to promulgate stricter environmental guidelines for OPIC in June 1997 that, among other things, require the agency to track and report on greenhouse gas emissions from its power projects and forbid it from backing projects in primary tropical forests or other ecologically fragile areas. Although the announcement was encouraging, substantial work remains to translate the general commitments it contained into specific, enforceable policies.[78]

The U.S. Export-Import Bank, which provides subsidized loans to other governments for the purchase of U.S. goods and services, has also taken steps in recent years to strengthen its environmental policies. It adopted revised environmental assessment criteria in 1994 that are more stringent than those of other bilateral export credit agencies. In May 1996, the bank announced that its environmental guidelines prohibited it from extending export credit support for China's Three Gorges project—a blow to companies such as the heavy equipment manufacturer Caterpillar, which had hoped to participate in the construction of the dam. The bank said it might reconsider if China improved its plans for protecting water quality and preserving endangered species. But in the meantime, the bank's counterparts in Canada, France, Germany, Japan, and Switzerland have stepped into the breach.   Stung by the experience, the United States is trying to persuade other donor countries to apply comparable environmental conditions to their bilateral export credit and investment promotion agencies.[79]

> **Environmental NGOs are now looking to private lenders and investors as potential allies.**

Although environmental NGOs have traditionally focused principally on public lending institutions as possible agents of change, they are now also looking to private lenders and investors as potential allies.   Unlike some governments, commercial banks require exhaustive studies of possible risks before making loans, a process known as "due diligence." Increasingly, banks are viewing environmental issues as an important consideration in this process.   The banks have a diverse range of concerns.   They worry that a hazardous waste dump will be discovered on a property that they lent money for, and that they will be held liable, as has happened in recent U.S. court cases.   They also fear that violations of environmental laws will lead to large financial penalties that will undermine a borrower's creditworthiness.   In the most extreme case, a project might be stopped altogether in the face of opposition from local citizens and environmental groups.[80]

"International commercial banks, whether they intend to be or not, are frequently very effective enforcers of local and international environmental requirements," maintains Bradford Gentry of Yale University.   "The level of scrutiny given to these issues by banks is often well above that of local environmental enforcement." Nonetheless, a recent study by the Washington, DC-based National Wildlife Federation found substantial room for progress: fewer than half of 51 financial institutions from 13 countries on four continents routinely conduct environmental due diligence on transactions other than those secured with real estate.[81]

In an effort to improve on this record, the United Nations Environment Programme (UNEP) launched an effort in 1992 to encourage major banks around the world to do a better job of incorporating environmental considerations into their lending programs. The initiative culminated in a "Statement by Banks on the Environment and Sustainable Development" that has so far been signed by 93 banks from 33 countries. The bankers underscored their expectation that borrowers must comply with "all applicable local, national, and international environmental regulations." The statement also includes a pledge on the part of signatory banks to update accounting procedures to adequately reflect environmental risks, and to develop banking products and services that promote environmental protection. Although laudable in its goals, the UNEP statement is short on specific commitments. The U.K.-based Green Alliance suggests strengthening the initiative by transforming the statement into a document whose expected standards of performance are clear enough to be subjected to the scrutiny of an audit.[82]

Stock market investors are also slowly beginning to show more interest in environmental questions. It used to be assumed that it was costly for companies to be good environmental stewards. But this view is giving ground to new evidence that environmentally progressive companies may in fact perform better, on average, than companies that are plagued by large environmental liabilities such as the threat of paying costly fines. A 1995 report by the Washington, DC-based Investor Responsibility Research Center compared the stock market performance of the 500 companies within the Standard & Poor's index, a group of 500 representative stocks and bonds. They divided the firms into "high-" and "low-"

polluting companies. Overall, the study found no penalty for investing in "green" portfolios, and in some cases it concluded that low-pollution portfolios actually demonstrated superior performance. A November 1996 study by the consulting firm ICF Kaiser was more bullish still. Its survey of more than 300 Standard & Poor's companies revealed that adopting a forward-looking environmental stance had a "significant and favorable impact" on a firm's value in the marketplace, as it reduced the perceived risk of investing in the company, and thus its cost of capital.[83]

As studies like these begin to accumulate, environmentally screened investment funds will likely grow in popularity. A frontrunner is the Global Environment Fund, a Washington-based investment fund manager founded in 1989. Loan guarantee agreements with OPIC have allowed the group to raise $190 million in investment capital from institutional investors for two Global Environment Emerging Markets Funds, which between them now have holdings in 10 countries in Africa, Asia, Eastern Europe, and Latin America. The principal focus of these funds is environmentally related infrastructure, including renewable energy projects and water and sewage treatment plants.[84]

Some $529 billion worth of investment—nearly 4 percent of all managed funds—is currently screened with some social criteria, according to the Washington, DC-based Social Investment Forum. An additional $736 billion—5 percent—is controlled by activist shareholders who try to influence the policies of the companies in which they own shares by participating in shareholder resolutions and proxy votes, among other techniques. In many cases, environmental criteria are one element in a broader social screen; in a few cases, funds are explicitly environmental in nature. The performance of these funds, like all investment funds, varies widely. Overall, however, the returns have been competitive. For instance, the Domini 400 Social, an index of socially screened firms, has outperformed the Standard & Poor 500 over much of the 1990s.[85]

Most screened funds are composed of companies listed on domestic stock exchanges, however, rather than interna-

tional ones.   One reason is the difficulty of tracking and
monitoring international companies.   Nonetheless, a few
screened funds are beginning to venture into international
markets.   Investment firms in emerging markets can themselves be active in this area: one of Thailand's leading investment houses offers a "Green Fund" that invests only in companies that they have screened for their environmental
management practices, with the help of independent groups
such as the Thailand Environment Institute.[86]

In an effort to scale up environmental private investing,
the IFC and the Global Environment Facility (GEF—a joint
undertaking of the U.N. Development Programme, the U.N.
Environment Programme, and the World Bank, and not to be
confused with the private Global Environment Fund discussed
above) are spearheading the creation of two venture capital
funds: a $20–25 million biodiversity fund for Latin America to
be called the Terra Capital Fund that will finance sustainable
forestry and agriculture programs and eco-tourism projects,
and a $210 million venture capital fund to promote energy
efficiency and renewable energy projects worldwide.[87]

The IFC is collaborating with the Global Environment
Facility to develop other green investment programs as well.
The goal is to devise financing mechanisms for projects that
are too small or unproven to attract standard IFC support or
other sources of international capital.   The average IFC loan
is $15 million, while many environmentally sound ventures
are looking for loans measured in thousands.   The new initiatives aim to demonstrate the viability of these smaller-
scale enterprises with a small injection of public funds so
that the industries will grow in size and be able to attract private capital on their own.[88]

One particularly promising IFC program channels
funds through environmental NGOs, nonprofit venture capital firms, and other intermediaries to a range of small-scale,
environmentally sound enterprises.   Projects in renewable
energy, energy efficiency, sustainable forestry and agriculture, and ecotourism are the funding targets. The program,
developed with a GEF grant, was originally capitalized at

$4.3 million. It has now been expanded with an additional $16.5 million and will involve some 100 different projects when fully up and running. Still, the whole program remains smaller than most individual IFC projects. And the IFC has been slow to devote its own resources to it, preferring to use the GEF's scarce funds instead.[89]

Governance for a Global Economy

The economic and environmental events in Asia over the last year demonstrate the need for reforms in global environmental governance. If we can see these crises as an opportunity, we may one day look back on them as useful warnings.

It has become fashionable to question whether national governments are still able to play their traditional regulatory role, given the growing power and nimbleness of international financial markets. In the environmental arena, at least, this concern is exaggerated. Countries have a number of environmental tools at their disposal if they choose to use them: they can strengthen traditional environmental laws and enforcement systems, for example, and implement innovations in national fiscal policy, such as reducing subsidies to environmentally harmful activities and taxing them instead. These sorts of policy reforms would change incentive structures throughout national economies, tipping the balance away from environmentally harmful investments and toward environmentally friendlier ones.[90]

Many developing countries have in fact made progress in strengthening environmental policies in recent years. Malaysia, for example, has implemented stringent effluent standards as well as fines to reduce pollution from the palm oil industry; China has cut its coal industry subsidies by more than half since the early 1990s, and has begun to experiment with pollution levies applied to wastewater, air pollutants, noise, and solid and radioactive waste; and Brazil, Costa Rica, and Honduras have begun to reform subsidies and other policies that contribute to deforestation. Similar initiatives are needed in other countries.[91]

Financial accounting rules and regulations also cry out for reform, if investors are to use their clout to push for environmental improvements. Companies operating in the United States are required to disclose large environmental liabilities such as hazardous waste sites on the forms they file with the Securities and Exchange Commission (SEC). But the information varies widely in quality, with many companies submitting no data at all. The reports are particularly sketchy about performance overseas: a recent survey by the Investor Responsibility Research Center found that 73 out of 97 companies with foreign operations failed to include information about their environmental track records abroad in publicly available documents such as SEC submissions.[92]

Developing countries have an opportunity to write environmental rules into the regulations governing their newly established stock markets. Thailand, for one, requires companies listed on the Stock Exchange of Thailand (SET) to undergo an environmental audit that includes an environmental impact assessment as well as a site visit. In addition, the SET has relaxed the stock-exchange-listing requirements for companies seeking finance for selected environmental control and prevention projects.[93]

Although national governments retain considerable scope for environmental innovation, the global nature of today's economy does mean that individual governments have less power than they once did to chart their own environmental course. The buying preferences of consumers continents away can determine the fate of a country's rainforest, for example, and concerns about international competitiveness are often used to block meaningful environmental reforms. Action on the international front is therefore essential.[94]

Many multinational corporations claim to adhere already to roughly uniform environmental policies and standards throughout their worldwide operations. And a number of international industry groups have now crafted voluntary codes of environmental conduct; many of them call for companies to approximate the standards of their home countries wherever they do business. In part, this is simply more practical than operating with a patchwork quilt of different practices around the world. Meeting international environmental criteria also allows companies to trumpet green credentials, which are of growing value in the international marketplace. An additional impetus for stricter internal corporate environmental policies is a desire to avoid adverse publicity—as well as a growing tendency for costly lawsuits to be filed in home-country courts for alleged environmental transgressions overseas.[95]

Over the last few years, numerous companies worldwide, many from developing countries, have applied for certification under the voluntary environmental management guidelines forged by the Geneva-based International Organization for Standardization (ISO), a worldwide federation of national standards-setting bodies. The first set of standards in the ISO 14,000 series, as it is known, was finalized in the fall of 1996. They cover internal management and auditing procedures—how, for instance, a company should monitor its pollution. These environmental management guidelines are not to be confused with actual performance standards that would specify, for example, what levels of pollution would be acceptable. But they are nonetheless a useful tool. ISO is now moving on to consider eco-labelling and life-cycle analysis (the evaluation of the environmental impacts of products from cradle to grave).[96]

Individual governments have less power than they once did to chart their own environmental course.

ISO's growing role is controversial given its narrow base: industry has been an active player from the beginning, but environmental groups did not participate until the negotiations were well along, and even then only on a limited basis. As the ISO process moves forward, it is important that wider constituencies be represented at the table. The Forest Stewardship Council and similar joint NGO-industry undertakings offer useful models.[97]

Beyond these independent initiatives, environmental considerations will need to be integrated into the official forums where the rules of international commerce are now being written. The discussions in 1993 on the North American Free Trade Agreement were one of the first attempts to put environmental issues high on the economic negotiating agenda. In this case, lobbying by environmental groups produced some concrete results, albeit relatively weak ones. The three NAFTA governments adopted an environmental "side agreement" that requires countries to enforce their own laws and provides for trade penalties if repeated efforts to persuade the offending countries to take action fail. NAFTA was also written with a clause that directs the parties not to lower their environmental standards—or their enforcement of them—in order to attract investment.[98]

NAFTA's environmental provisions and the side agreement have raised the visibility of the region's shared environmental problems and generated pressure for more responsible practices. Yet much room for progress remains, particularly in the heavily polluted border area: a 1995 report found that roughly a quarter of maquiladora hazardous waste—some 44 tons daily—could not be accounted for, presumably because it is dumped in ditches.[99]

At least one other major trade regime appears to be following NAFTA's lead, although in its own way. The Asia-Pacific Economic Cooperation (APEC) forum is a loose coalition of 18 Pacific Rim states, including China, Indonesia, Japan, and the United States. Between them, these countries are home to 40 percent of the world's population. Rhetorically at least, APEC has put the cause of sustainable development high on its agenda, focusing in particular on the challenge of creating sustainable cities, cleaner industries, and healthier oceans and fisheries. In addition, APEC's "Non-binding Investment Principles" contain an environmental provision similar to NAFTA's investment clause.[100]

In 1998, another major international economic agreement is being negotiated with insufficient regard for its environmental effects—despite the efforts of environmental groups. The Organisation for Economic Co-operation and Development (OECD), a body composed mainly of western industrial governments, is in the process of negotiating a Multilateral Agreement on Investment (MAI) intended to lower obstacles to foreign investment. In its current form, the agreement contains a number of provisions that could constrain the ability of countries to minimize the environmental damage and social disruption of foreign investment projects. At the same time, it lacks provisions that would require investors to meet high environmental standards.

The IMF needs an injection of environmental sensitivity.

Though negotiated by OECD members, participation in the treaty will be open to other countries. And developments in the OECD often lay the groundwork for future accords at the World Trade Organization.[101]

Like international trade agreements, the core principle behind the MAI is the idea that signatories should apply the same conditions to foreign companies that they impose on domestic ones. If approved without substantial revision, the MAI could sweep away numerous existing environmental protections that contradict this tenet, such as a law in Taiwan that forbids foreign investment in "highly polluting industries," one in Columbia that prohibits foreign investment in the processing and disposal of toxic and radioactive wastes produced overseas, and limits that Honduras imposes on foreign investment in commercial fishing.[102]

The International Monetary Fund is yet another economic institution that needs an injection of environmental sensitivity. The IMF's prominent role in the Asian economic crisis is demonstrating the organization's power, while at the same time stirring controversy as to the wisdom of its financial advice. Little understood, however, are the profound effects that its economic recommendations have on the ecological health of recipient countries. The IMF urges countries to boost exports in order to generate foreign exchange with which to pay back debts: this creates pressure on them to liquidate natural assets in order to come up with the money. The Fund also often advises countries to cut government spending, which can mean that the budgets of already overburdened environment and natural resource management ministries are cut to bare-bones levels.[103]

Although many IMF policies contribute to environmental destruction, the agency's influence could be harnessed on behalf of needed reforms, such as reducing environmentally harmful subsidies or implementing environmental taxes. In a few recent cases, the Fund has tried to use its clout to halt the destruction of natural capital. It suspended loans to Cambodia in 1996 and 1997 after government officials awarded logging concessions to foreign firms that threatened to open up the country's entire remaining forest area to exploitation—while funneling tens of millions of dollars into the bank accounts of the corrupt officials. And a loan to Mauritania reportedly included provisions to encourage better management of the country's fisheries. These were steps forward for the IMF, but they remain the exception rather than the rule.[104]

While the last several years have seen a steady strengthening of global economic governance, environmental governance continues to lag behind. Nonetheless, a number of international agreements hold promise as tools for pointing global commerce in a more environmentally sound direction. Two environmental treaties—the 1992 U.N. Convention on Biological Diversity and the 1992 U.N. Framework Convention on Climate Change, including its 1997 Kyoto Protocol—could play particularly strong roles, if full use is made of them. The biodiversity convention, which has now been ratified by 169 countries, requires signatories to forge national strategies aimed at preserving biological wealth. It also mandates environmental impact assessments of proposed projects "likely to have significant adverse effects on biological diversity with a view to avoiding or minimizing such effects." The climate change treaty, ratified by 167 countries, commits all signatories to adopt climate-sensitive national policies, although it specifies no specific carbon emissions targets for developing countries. The Kyoto Protocol reaffirms these earlier pledges and creates a "Clean Development Mechanism" to encourage private investment in the developing world in climate-friendly energy and forestry projects.[105]

Looming on the horizon is the question of whether the United Nations should be charged with developing baseline environmental standards for industry comparable to those that the International Labour Organisation drafts on matters such as workplace safety and child labor. This effort could build on the World Bank's environmental policies and guidelines, which are already a common point of reference for private investors. It could also draw on an existing UNEP initiative in which task forces with industry representation produce technical guidelines, case studies, and examples of "best practice" for diverse industries such as textiles, electronics, and pulp and paper.[106]

For any international standards to be effective, they ought to meet three basic principles: they should be minimum standards that companies and countries are free to exceed if they wish; they must be set high enough to have a real impact; and they need to be developed in an open and inclusive process to build a strong consensus in support of them.

The need for accountability suggests a final governance challenge: democratizing decisionmaking in a world where remote investors and often-impenetrable international institutions are increasingly calling the shots. Already, a grassroots citizens' movement is rapidly gaining strength in many parts of the world as a powerful countervailing force. In a victory for local environmentalists, in March 1997 the Chilean Supreme Court overturned the national environment agency's approval of a plan to allow the Trillium Corporation (based in Bellingham, Washington) to log an ancient beech forest. In another recent triumph, a coalition of academics, ecologists, indigenous groups, and opposition politicians joined forces in Venezuela to protest a government plan to open an ecologically rich forest reserve to gold mining. In November 1997, the Venezuelan Supreme Court banned the granting of any concessions in this area—at least for the time being.[107]

Environmental activists are increasingly interlinked internationally, with the Internet facilitating well-coordinated campaigns that span the globe. Their campaigns influence and occasionally halt environmentally damaging projects through multifaceted efforts involving traditional grassroots tactics as well as direct lobbying of corporations, private investors, and international institutions.[108]

Perhaps the strongest proof of the growing strength of the citizens movement is the seriousness with which the international business community views it. A recent report by the Control Risks Group, a London-based firm that advises businesses on political and security risks, describes "the pressure on companies, wherever they operate, to adopt the highest international environmental, labour and ethical standards." According to the report, "heightened international scrutiny means that perceived transgressors truly have 'no hiding place'."[109]

If international companies have 'no hiding place', it is as much a reflection of the urgency of the challenge before us as it is a commentary on the influence of environmental groups. The global economy is bumping up against immutable ecological limits, placing us all in a race against time. Only by shifting private investment capital out of environmentally damaging activities and into the technologies and enterprises of tomorrow will it be possible to turn the tide of global ecological decline.

Notes

1. World Bank, *The East Asian Miracle: Economic Growth and Public Policy* (New York: Oxford University Press, 1993); Paul Krugman, "First: Whatever Happened to the Asian Miracle?" *Fortune*, 18 August 1997; Peter Montagnon, "Economies: Asia's Endangered Tigers," *Financial Times*, 30 August 1997; information on Indonesian fires, including economic loss estimate, from Nigel Dudley, *The Year the World Caught Fire*, World Wide Fund for Nature (WWF), International Discussion Paper (Gland, Switzerland: WWF, December 1997).

2. The World Bank classifies all low- and middle-income countries as developing, including all of Africa and Latin America, and selected countries in Asia and the Pacific, the Caribbean, Eastern Europe, and the Middle East. This definition is used in all figures, tables, and textual references in this paper. Developing countries still receive only a relatively small share of total international private capital flows—37 percent of all foreign direct investment (FDI) inflows in 1996, per United Nations Conference on Trade and Development (UNCTAD), *World Investment Report 1997* (New York: United Nations, 1997). Private capital flows to developing countries from 1990 through 1996 from World Bank, *Global Development Finance 1997: Volume 1* (Washington, DC: 1997). 1996 number is preliminary. Economic growth rates from International Monetary Fund (IMF), *World Economic Outlook*, October 1996 (Washington, DC: 1996); private capital flows in 1997 a preliminary estimate from IMF, *World Economic Outlook*, Interim Assessment (Washington, DC: December 1997). World Bank figures for 1997 were not available as this report went to press; IMF and World Bank estimates have been roughly comparable in recent years. Figure 1 is based on World Bank, op. cit. this note; World Bank, *Debtor Reporting System*, electronic database, Washington, DC, as of 30 July 1997; and IMF, op. cit., this note (for 1997). 1996 and 1997 numbers are preliminary.

3. Jeff Gerth and Richard W. Stevenson, "Poor Oversight Said to Imperil World Banking," *New York Times*, 22 December 1997; George Soros, "Asia's Crisis Demands a Rethink of International Regulation," *Financial Times*, 31 December 1997.

4. IMF, October 1996, op. cit. note 2; Asian Development Bank (ADB), *Emerging Asia: Changes and Challenges* (Manila: 1997); World Resources Institute (WRI), United Nations Environment Programme (UNEP), United Nations Development Programme (UNDP), and World Bank, *World Resources 1996-97* (New York and Oxford: Oxford University Press, 1996); Ashley T. Mattoon, "Paper Profits," and Anne Platt McGinn, "The (Aqua)cultural Revolution," *World Watch*, forthcoming, March/April 1998; Molly O'Meara, "The Risks of Disrupting Climate," *World Watch*, November/December 1997.

5. Organisation for Economic Co-operation and Development (OECD), *Economic Globalization and the Environment* (Paris: 1997); Richard J. Barnet and John Cavanagh, *Global Dreams: Imperial Corporations and the New World*

Order (New York: Simon and Schuster, 1994); Lester R. Brown, "The Future of Growth," in Lester R. Brown, Christopher Flavin, Hilary French et al., *State of the World 1998* (New York: W. W. Norton & Company, 1998).

6.   OECD, op. cit. note 5.

7.   Development assistance spending decline and aid versus private flows based on World Bank, *Global Development Finance*, op. cit. note 2. 1996 numbers are preliminary estimates. Reasons for aid's decline from OECD, *Development Cooperation:1996 Report* (Paris: 1997).

8.   Carbon emissions based on G. Marland, R.J. Andres, T.A. Boden, and C. Johnston, *Global, Regional, and National CO_2 Emission Estimates from Fossil Fuel Burning, Cement Production, and Gas Flaring: 1751-1995* (Oak Ridge, TN: Carbon Dioxide Information Analysis Center, Oak Ridge National Laboratory, January 1998), and on British Petroleum, *BP Statistical Review of World Energy* (London: Group Media & Publications, 1997); species extinction rate is a Worldwatch estimate based on Nigel Stork, "Measuring Global Biodiversity and Its Decline," in Marjorie L. Reaka-Kudla, Don E. Wilson, and Edward O. Wilson, eds., *Biodiversity II: Understanding and Protecting Our Biological Resources* (Washington, DC: Joseph Henry Press, 1997).

9.   World Bank, *Private Capital Flows to Developing Countries* (New York: Oxford University Press, 1997).

10.   Major source countries from UNCTAD, op. cit. note 2, and from David Hedley, Institute of International Finance, Inc. (IIF), discussion with Payal Sampat, Worldwatch Institute, 18 September 1997; Jacques de Larosière, "Financing Development in a World of Private Capital Flows: The Challenge for Multilateral Development Banks in Working with the Private Sector," the Per Jacobsson Lecture, Washington, DC, 29 September 1996; World Bank, op. cit. note 9.

11.   Table 1 based on World Bank, *Global Development Finance*, op. cit. note 2, World Bank, *World Development Indicators on CD-ROM* (Washington, DC: 1997), and United Nations Population Fund, *The State of World Population 1996* (New York: 1996). Figure 2 based on World Bank, *Global Development Finance*, op. cit. note 2, as well as examples interspersed throughout the paper. Additional examples from the following sources: James Brooke, "Mining Companies Increasingly Look Abroad," *New York Times*, 13 August 1996; Travis Q. Lyday, "The Mineral Industry of Papua New Guinea," in United States Geological Survey, *Minerals Yearbook, Volume III—Area Reports: International* (Reston, VA: 1996); Conservation International, "Natural Resource Extraction in the Latin American Tropics: A New Wave of Investment Poses Challenges for Biodiversity Conservation," draft, Washington, DC, January 1998; "Battle for Strategic Positions in Zaire," *Financial Times*, 23 April 1997; Howard French, "The Great Gold Rush in Zaire," *New York Times*, 18 April 1997; Pacific Environment and Resources Center (PERC) and Friends of the Earth U.S. (FOE), "Case Studies: OPIC Horror Shows," information sheet, (Washington, DC: April 1997).

12. Based on World Bank, *World Development Indicators*, op. cit. note 11, and World Bank, *Global Development Finance*, op. cit. note 2.

13. Table 2 based on World Bank, *Global Development Finance*, op. cit. note 2.

14. FDI numbers from World Bank, *Global Development Finance*, op. cit. note 2 (total excludes some countries for which no data are given); gross domestic investment numbers based on World Bank, *World Development Indicators*, op. cit. note 11.

15. R.R. Palmer and Joel Colton, *A History of the Modern World* (New York: Alfred A. Knopf, Fifth Edition, 1978); Gerald M. Meier, *Leading Issues in Economic Development*, Sixth Edition (New York: Oxford University Press, 1995); Theodore Panayotou, "The Role of the Private Sector in Sustainable Infrastructure Development," in Luis Gomez-Echeverri, ed., *Bridges to Sustainability: Business and Government Working Together for a Better Environment*, Yale School of Forestry and Environmental Studies Bulletin Series, Number 101 (New Haven, CT: Yale University, 1997).

16. World Bank, *Global Development Finance*, op. cit. note 2. The "services" sector is also known as the "tertiary" sector.

17. U.S. Foreign Direct Investment outflows and Table 3 based on U.S. Department of Commerce, *Survey of Current Business*, July 1993 and September 1997.

18. China from *Almanac of China's Foreign Economic Relations and Trade* (various issues), supplied by Masataka Fujita, UNCTAD, letter to Payal Sampat, Worldwatch Institute, 12 December 1997; Brazil, Chile, and Table 4 based on Inter-American Development Bank (IDB)/Institute for European-Latin Relations (IRELA), *Latin America: The New Economic Climate* (Madrid: IRELA, 1996); Alejandro C. Vera-Vassallo, "Foreign Investment and Competitive Development in Latin America and the Caribbean," *Cepal Review 60*, December 1996; Botswana from "African Investment: New Signs of Vitality," press release (Geneva: UNCTAD, 1 May 1997); Tunisia from World Bank, *World Debt Tables 1996, Volume 1* (Washington, DC: 1996), and from UNCTAD, *Foreign Direct Investment in Africa 1995* (New York: United Nations, 1995).

19. Ranking of companies and share of holdings in developing world from UNCTAD, op. cit. note 2; Exxon, *Annual Report 1996*, <http://www.exxon.com/exxoncorp/shareholder_info/annual_96>, viewed 24 September 1997; Royal Dutch/Shell, *Annual Report 1996*, <http://194.93.128.253/Annual_Report/index.html>, viewed 24 September 1997.

20. UNCTAD, op. cit. note 2.

21. World Bank, *Global Development Finance*, op. cit. note 2; stock markets from Ted C. Fishman, "The Joys of Global Investment," *Harper's Magazine*, February 1997; emerging market funds from World Bank, op. cit. note 9; sectors from various investment fund prospectuses; history from A.G. Kenwood and A.L. Loughheed, *The Growth of the International Economy 1820-1990* (London and New York: Routledge, Third Edition, 1992).

22. De Larosière, op. cit. note 10; Asian and Mexican crashes referred to in IIF, *Capital Flows to Emerging Market Economies: Update*, biannual report (Washington, DC: 11 September 1997); portfolio equity and bonds from World Bank, *Global Development Finance*, op. cit. note 2; IMF, Interim Assessment, op. cit. note 2.

23. World Bank, *Global Development Finance*, op. cit. note 2; IIF, op. cit. note 22.

24. Palmer and Colton, op. cit. note 15; de Larosière, op. cit. note 10.

25. De Larosière, op. cit. note 10; World Bank, *Global Development Finance*, op. cit. note 2; "Honeymoon over for Asian Banks as Regional Crisis Bites," Agence France Press English Wire, 9 November 1997; John Ridding, "Hong Kong: Braced as Asia Storms Swirl," *Financial Times*, 9 January 1998.

26. Vera-Vassallo, op. cit. note 18; IDB/IRELA, op. cit. note 18.

27. Table 5 and metals exploration numbers based on Metals Economic Group (MEG), *Strategic Report* (Halifax, NS, Canada: November/December 1991), and MEG, "Latin America Tops Exploration Spending for the Fourth Year," press release (Halifax, NS, Canada: 16 October 1997); gold exploration figures from MEG, *Strategic Report* September/October 1997 (Halifax, NS, Canada: 1997); prospecting shift from William C. Symonds, "All that Glitters is Not Bre-X," *Business Week*, 19 May 1997.

28. Christine A. Adamec, "Face Forward," *Mining Voice*, May/June 1996; 70 countries from Symonds, op. cit. note 27; gold-to-waste ratio from John E. Young, "Gold Production at Record High," in Lester R. Brown, Hal Kane, and David Malin Roodman, *Vital Signs 1994* (New York: W.W. Norton & Company, 1994), based on U.S. Bureau of Mines data; indigenous peoples figure from Roger Moody, "The Lure of Gold—How Golden Is the Future?" Panos Media Briefing No. 19 (London: Panos Institute, May 1996). For more on the environmental and social impacts of mining around the world, see John E. Young, *Mining the Earth*, Worldwatch Paper 109 (Washington, DC: Worldwatch Institute, July 1992).

29. Oil and gas reserves from Hossein Razavi, "Financing Oil and Gas Projects in Developing Countries," *Finance and Development*, June 1996; regions from Jonathan Friedland, "Oil Companies Strive to Turn a New Leaf to Save Rain Forest," *Wall Street Journal*, 17 July 1997, from Patricia M. Carey, "Prospecting for Project Finance," *Infrastructure Finance*, April/May 1995, and from Geoff B. Kleburtz et al., Salomon Brothers Inc., "97 E&P Spending: Strongest Outlook in Nine Years," *World Oil*, February 1997.

30. UNCTAD, *World Investment Report 1992* (New York: United Nations, 1992); Côte d'Ivoire figure from Nigel Dudley, Jean-Paul Jeanrenaud, and Francis Sullivan, *Bad Harvest: The Timber Trade and the Degradation of the World's Forests* (London: WWF and Earthscan Publications, 1995); role of Japanese companies from Joshua Karliner, *The Corporate Planet: Ecology and Politics in the Age of Globalization* (San Francisco: Sierra Club Books, 1997).

31. Jonathan Friedland, "Troubled at Home, Asian Timber Firms Set Sights on Amazon," *Wall Street Journal*, 11 November 1996; Gilney Viana, Congressional Representative, Brazil, *Initiatives in the Defense of the Amazon Rainforest* (Brasília: September 1996); Cheri Sugal, Conservation International, discussion with author, 14 January 1998; Nigel Sizer, *Profit without Plunder: Reaping Revenue from Guyana's Tropical Forests without Destroying Them* (Washington, DC: WRI, September 1996); Julia Preston, "It's Indians vs. Loggers in Nicaragua," *New York Times*, 25 June 1996; Nigel Sizer and Richard Rice, *Backs to the Wall in Suriname: Forest Policy in a Country in Crisis* (Washington, DC: WRI, April 1995); Greenpeace International, *Logging the Planet: Asian Companies Marching Across Our Last Forest Frontiers*, (Amsterdam: 1997); last untouched forests from Dirk Bryant, Daniel Nielsen, and Laura Tangley, *The Last Frontier Forests: Ecosystems & Economies on the Edge* (Washington, DC: WRI, 1997).

32. "Changes Ongoing in World Markets," *International Woodfiber Report*, from <http://www.pponline.com/db-area/wood-rpt>, viewed 18 January 1998; John Ross, "Treasure of the Costa Grande," *Sierra*, July/August 1996; Charles W. Thurston, "Brazil Upgrading Its Pulp Capacity," *Journal of Commerce*, 8 October 1997; "Go South Young Man," *Financial Times*, 1 October 1997; information on Chile from Nigel Dudley, Sue Stolton, and Jean-Paul Jeanrenaud, *Pulp Fact: the Environmental and Social Impacts of the Pulp and Paper Industry* (Gland, Switzerland: WWF International, 1995) and Ricardo Carrere and Larry Lohmann, *Pulping the South: Industrial Tree Plantations and the World Paper Economy* (London: Zed Books Ltd., 1996).

33. Role of international investment in agriculture from United Nations Centre on Transnational Corporations data cited in Karliner, op. cit. note 30; Atossa Soltani and Tracey Osborne, *Arteries for Global Trade, Consequences for Amazonia* (Malibu, CA: Amazon Watch, April 1997); Peter May, Ana Célia Castro, and Antonio Barros de Castro, "Expansion and Technical Innovation in Brazil's Soybean-Based Agroindustrial Complex," in Bradford S. Gentry, ed., *Private Capital Flows and the Environment: Lessons from Latin America* (Cheltenham, UK: Edward Elgar Press, forthcoming); "Government, Environmentalists Up in Arms over U.S. Firm's Logging of Endangered Forests," *International Environment Reporter*, 17 September 1997.

34. Anne Platt McGinn, "Promoting Sustainable Fisheries," in Brown, Flavin, French et al., op. cit. note 5; Gareth Porter, "Euro-African Fishing Agreements: Subsidizing Overfishing in African Waters," in Scott Burns, ed., *Subsidies and Depletion of World Fisheries: Case Studies* (Washington, DC: World Wildlife Fund's Endangered Seas Campaign, April 1997); Okechukwu C. Iheduru, "The Political Economy of Euro-African Fishing Agreements," *The Journal of Developing Areas*, October 1995.

35. Debt from World Bank, *Global Development Finance, Volume 2* (Washington, DC: 1997); Senegal figure from Stephen Buckley, "Senegalese Fish for a Living in Seas Teeming with Industrial Rivals," *International Herald Tribune*, 4 November 1997; Suriname figure from Sizer and Rice, op. cit. note 31; ongoing rumors from Sugal, op. cit. note 31.

36. Jeffrey D. Sachs and Andrew M. Warner, *Natural Resource Abundance and Economic Growth*, Development Discussion Paper No. 517a (Cambridge, MA: Harvard Institute for International Development, October 1995); ADB, op. cit. note 4; linkages from Philip Daniel, "Economic Policy in Mineral-Exporting Countries: What Have We Learned?" in John E. Tilton, ed., *Mineral Wealth and Economic Development* (Washington, DC: Resources for the Future, 1992); failure of developing countries to reap maximum benefits from natural resources from David Smith, Vice-Dean, Harvard Law School, discussion with author, 5 January 1998.

37. Walter V. Reid et al., *Biodiversity Prospecting: Using Genetic Resources for Sustainable Development* (Washington, DC: WRI, May 1993).

38. Ibid.; Jeffrey A. McNeely, "Achieving Financial Sustainability in Biodiversity Conservation Programs," in *Investing in Biodiversity Conservation*, Workshop Proceedings, IDB, July 1997.

39. McNeely, op. cit. note 38; Julie M. Feinsilver, "Biodiversity Prospecting: A New Panacea for Development?" *Cepal Review 60*, December 1996; Layla Hughes, Conservation International, letter to Payal Sampat, Worldwatch Institute, 1 October 1997.

40. Sizer, op. cit. note 31; export revenue figures from Douglas Southgate, *Alternatives for Habitat Protection and Rural Income Generation*, (Washington, DC: IDB, March 1997); role for international investment in ecotourism from Katrina Brandon, *Ecotourism and Conservation: A Review of Key Issues* (Washington, DC: World Bank, April 1996).

41. Cheri Sugal, "Labeling Wood," *World Watch*, September/October 1996; doubling between 1994 and 1996 from World Wildlife Fund-UK, *World Wildlife Fund Guide to Forest Certification 1997*, Forests for Life Campaign (Godalming, Surrey, U.K.: 1997); total timber trade from U.N. Food and Agriculture Organization, *FAO Forests Products Yearbook 1983-1994* (Rome: 1996); Rainforest Alliance, "SmartWood List of Certified Operations," fact-sheet (New York: September 1997); idem, SmartWood Program, "Public

Certification Summary Report for Natural Forest Assessment of Mil Madeireira Itacoatiara Ltd." (New York: August 1997).

42. Andrew Wheat, "Toxic Bananas," *Multinational Monitor*, September 1996; Andrea Spencer-Cooke, "Eco-Labeling goes Bananas," *Tomorrow*, September-October 1997; Anne Platt McGinn, "A Private-Sector Sustainable Fishing Initiative," *World Watch*, September/October 1996.

43. ADB, op. cit. note 4.

44. The U.S. Department of Commerce includes food products, chemicals, machinery, paper products, electronics equipment, and several other industries in its category of manufacturing, per *Survey of Current Business*, March 1995. The United Nations Industry and Development Organization (UNIDO) uses a similar definition, per UNIDO, *Industrial Development: Global Report 1996* (Oxford: Oxford University Press, 1996). Information on relative labor intensity and environmental sensitivity of various industries from Michael Renner, *Jobs in a Sustainable Economy*, Worldwatch Paper 104 (Washington, DC: Worldwatch Institute, September 1991).

45. Share of developing countries in production of various industries from data provided by Gerhard Magreiter, UNIDO, letter to Payal Sampat, Worldwatch Institute, 3 October 1997.

46. World Bank, *Global Development Finance*, op. cit. note 2; U.S. Department of Commerce, September 1997, op. cit. note 17.

47. Bradford S. Gentry and Daniel C. Esty, "Private Capital Flows: New and Additional Resources for Sustainable Development," in Gomez-Echeverri, op. cit. note 15; OECD, op. cit. note 5.

48. Howard Hu, "Exporting Hazardous Industries, Products, and Wastes," *Our Planet*, no. 6, 1997; Carlos Plazola, Silicon Valley Toxics Coalition, "The Globalization of High Tech: Environmental Injustices Plague Industry," <http://www.corpwatch.org/feature/hitech/global.html>, viewed 15 September 1997; "Global Manufacturing and Assembly Facilities for the Computer Manufacturing Industry," Silicon Valley Toxics Coalition, San Jose, CA, April 1997.

49. For a full though somewhat dated discussion of the role of environmental factors in companies' location decisions, see H. Jeffrey Leonard, *Pollution and the Struggle for the World Product* (Cambridge, U.K.: Cambridge University Press, 1988); on North American Free Trade Agreement (NAFTA) debate's focus on the border area, see, for example, John Holusha, "Trade Pact May Intensify Problems at the Border," *New York Times*, 20 August 1992; number of manufacturing plants from Gary Clyde Hufbacher and Jeffrey J. Schott, *North American Free Trade: Issues and Recommendations* (Washington, DC: Institute for International Economics, 1992); Mexicali from Roberto Sanchez, "Health and Environmental Risks of the Maquiladora in Mexico,"

Natural Resources Journal, winter 1990; S.J.Lewis et al., *Border Trouble: Rivers in Peril* (Boston: National Toxics Campaign Fund, 1991).

50. Jason Abbott, "Export Processing Zones and the Developing World," *Contemporary Review*, no. 1576, 1997; Cavite information from Keith B. Richburg, "Under Southeast Asia's Haze: More Bad Air," *Washington Post*, 5 October 1997; Chinese accusation from Xia Guang, "Pollution by Foreign Firms Rises," *China Environment News*, 15 February 1997.

51. McDonald's quote from Stefan Lovgren, "Instead of Aid, Trade," *U.S. News & World Report*, 13 October 1997.

52. Keith Bradsher, "In the Biggest, Booming Cities, A Car Population Problem," *New York Times*, 11 May 1997; Rebecca Blumenstein, "GM is Building Plants in Developing Nations to Woo New Markets," *Wall Street Journal*, 8 August 1997; Manjeet Kripalani, "A Traffic Jam of Auto Makers," *Business Week*, 5 August 1996.

53. Ernst Von Weizäcker, Amory B. Lovins, and L. Hunter Lovins, *Factor Four: Doubling Wealth, Halving Resource Use* (London: Earthscan Publications Ltd., 1997); David Wheeler and Paul Martin, "Prices, Policies, and International Diffusion of Clean Technology: The Case of Wood Pulp Production," in Patrick Low, ed., *International Trade and the Environment*, World Bank Discussion Papers (Washington, DC: World Bank, 1992); Pamela Stedman-Edwards et al., *The Private Sector in Latin America: Implications for the Environment and Sustainable Development* (Washington, DC: World Wildlife Fund, July 1997); Bradford S. Gentry, *Private Investment and the Environment*, Discussion Paper 11 (New York: UNDP, undated); Bradford S. Gentry and Lisa Fernandez, "Mexican Steel," in Gentry, ed., op.cit. note 33.

54. Steven Nadel et al., *Lighting Energy Efficiency in China: Current Status, Future Directions* (Washington, DC: American Council for an Energy-Efficient Economy, May 1997); Rakesh Bakshi, "Country Survey: India," *Wind Directions*, April 1997; wind energy capacity from Birger T. Madsen, BTM Consult, Ringkobing, Denmark, letter to Christopher Flavin, Worldwatch Institute, 7 January 1998.

55. Safe water from UNDP, *Human Development Report 1997* (New York: Oxford University Press, 1997); electricity from World Bank, *Rural Energy and Development: Improving Energy Supplies for Two Billion People* (Washington, DC: 1996); sanitation from UNICEF, *The Progress of Nations 1997* (New York: United Nations, 1997).

56. International Finance Corporation (IFC), *Financing Private Infrastructure* (Washington, DC: World Bank and IFC, 1996); World Bank, *Global Development Finance*, op. cit. note 2. These World Bank figures exclude FDI due to methodological complications.

57. ADB, op. cit. note 4; Theodore Panayotou, "Asia in the 21st Century: Can It Grow Cleaner as It Grows Richer?" unpublished paper based on "Environment and Natural Resources," draft, ADB, op. cit. note 4.

58. Growth of developing-country power sector from International Energy Agency, *World Energy Outlook: 1996 Edition* (Paris: OECD, 1996).

59. Interest of international investors from Craig S. Smith, "China Experiments with Open Bidding to Break Logjam on Power Projects," *Wall Street Journal*, 6 December 1996, and from Henny Sender, "Fired Up," *Far Eastern Economic Review*, 16 January 1997; number of power plants to be built based on projections provided by Shi Dazhen, President of the State Power Corporation of China, in "Reform and Development of China's Power Industry," presented to CERA *Global Power Forum Summit*, February 13, 1997; "Authorities Reveal 3 Million Deaths Linked to Illness from Air Pollution," *International Environment Reporter*, 30 October 1996; China carbon emissions from Seth Dunn, "Carbon Emissions Set New Record," in Lester R. Brown, Michael Renner, and Christopher Flavin, *Vital Signs 1997* (New York: W.W. Norton & Company, 1997), based on data from Oak Ridge National Laboratory and British Petroleum; projections for 2010 are a Worldwatch estimate based on current carbon emissions growth rates; Paiton plant from World Bank, *Global Development Finance*, op. cit. note 2, and IFC, op. cit. note 56.

60. "Survey: Power Generation," *Financial Times*, 19 June 1997; N. Vasuki Rao, "Power Transmission Open to Private Funds in India," *Journal of Commerce*, 24 January 1997; "Brazil: Enron, Amoco Bid for Thermal Power Plant at Cuiaba," *South American Business Info.*, 14 May 1997, retrieved through DIALOG online database, 23 January 1998; Kevin G. Hall, "El Salvador Set to Launch Bidding on Power Grids," *Journal of Commerce*, 20 February 1997; Kenneth Cooper, "Wattage to India," *Washington Post*, 5 February 1996; "Indonesia Picks Gas over Nuclear," *Journal of Commerce*, 7 August 1997; "Nissho Iwai, ABB to Build Power Plants in Mexico," Agence France Press English Wire, 9 September 1997; Jeremy Grant, "Vietnam Faces the Prospect of Power Crunch Next Year," *Financial Times*, 25 July 1997; Soltani and Osborne, op. cit. note 33; quote from Jonathan Friedland, "In This 'Great Game,' No Holds Are Barred," *Wall Street Journal*, 14 August 1996; Michael S. Lelyveld, "Central Asia, Mideast Generate Gas, Power Deals," *Journal of Commerce*, 26 February 1997; "Thai National Environment Board Approves EIA for Gas Pipeline, With Conditions," *International Environment Reporter*, 2 April 1997.

61. Electricity to be supplied from James Harding, "China: More Winners Emerge in Three Gorges Scramble," *Financial Times*, 20 August 1997; flooding and resettlement numbers are U.S. Export-Import Bank estimates cited in "Ex-Im Bank Turns Down Requests to Consider Three Gorges Lending," *International Environment Reporter*, 12 June 1996; financing plans from "Contest Hots Up for Huge Yangtze Power Contracts," *Financial Times*, 25 July 1997; International Rivers Network, "Full-Page *NY Times* Ad Urges US Investors Not to Fund Three Gorges Dam; Editorial Also Opposes US Support," press release (Berkeley, CA: 20 November 1997).

62. James Kynge, "Malaysia Appeal Court Clears Way for Dam Project," *Financial Times*, 18 February 1997; "Financial Backers of Bakun Dam Agree to Cancel Share Rights Issue," *International Environment Reporter*, 25 June 1997; "Bakun Dam Construction Delayed Until Country Recovers From Economic Crisis," *International Environment Reporter*, 17 September 1997; "Some Component Works of Bakun Project to Continue," *The Star* (Kuala Lumpur, Malaysia), 22 January 1998, posted on International Rivers Network e-mail listserve, 22 January 1998.

63. Triodos Bank from Christopher Flavin and Molly O'Meara, "Financing Solar Electricity," *World Watch*, May/June 1997; Solar Electric Light Company, "International Solar Energy Company Launched to Provide Solar Electricity to Developing Countries," press release, (Washington, DC: 1 October 1997); "Solar Century to Promote Global PV Markets," *Business and the Environment*, September 1997; Casper Henderson, "The Solar Revival," *Financial Times*, 3 July 1996; Enron Corp., "Amoco/Enron Solar Wins Contract to Build Largest Photovoltaic Solar Power Plant in the United States," press release (Houston, TX: 28 October 1996); Carol Hensley, spokesperson, Enron Corp., discussion with Payal Sampat, Worldwatch Institute, 24 October 1997.

64. Rogati Kayani and Andrew Dymond, *Options for Rural Telecommunications Development*, World Bank Technical Paper No. 359 (Washington, DC: World Bank, 1997); Lisa Sykes, "Hanging On for the Phone," *New Scientist*, 14 June 1997; "Global Group Seeks Ways to Narrow Info Gap," *World Bank News*, 10 July 1997.

65. Figure of $600 billion from Ismail Serageldin, *Toward Sustainable Management of Water Resources* (Washington, DC: World Bank, 1995); Sandra Postel, *Last Oasis*, rev. ed. (New York: W.W. Norton & Company, 1997); Gentry, op. cit. note 53.

66. Postel, op. cit. note 65; Carl Frankel, "Heaven Can Wait," *Tomorrow*, September/October 1997; IFC, op. cit. note 56.

67. IFC, op. cit. note 56; Emanuel Idelovitch and Klas Ringskog, *Private Participation in Water Supply and Sanitation in Latin America* (Washington, DC: World Bank, 1995).

68. Environmental Business International, Inc., San Diego, CA, "The Global Environmental Market and United States Environmental Industry Competitiveness," undated; R. Rajagopal, "India Attracts the World's Environmental Companies," *Chemical Engineering*, 1 January 1996, posted on India News Network Digest, e-mail listserve, 11 October 1997.

69. Michelle Chan, *Anatomy of a Deal: A Handbook of International Project Finance* (Washington, DC: FOE, April 1996).

70. Description of World Bank private sector operations from World Bank, *The World Bank: Annual Report 1997* (Washington, DC: 1997); ratio of loans to private funds from IFC, "Investing in Development," Corporate Relations Office Slide Presentation, Washington, DC, 1997; MIGA numbers from Multilateral Investment Guarantee Agency, *MIGA Business Profile 1997* (Washington, DC: World Bank Group, August 1997); 10 percent figure from World Bank, *The World Bank: Annual Report 1995* (Washington, DC: 1995); Paul Lewis, "New World Bank: Consultant to Third World Investors," *New York Times*, 27 April 1995.

71. IFC, "FY97 IFC Financing by Sector," Corporate Relations Office Slide Presentation, Washington, DC, 1997; Friends of the Earth-U.S., "IFC Investments in Latin America and Caribbean," "IFC Investments in Central Asia, Middle East, North Africa," "IFC Investments in Asia," and "IFC Investments in Sub-Saharan Africa," fact sheets (Washington, DC: undated).

72. For a description of World Bank environmental policies and guidelines, see World Bank, *Environment Matters: Annual Review* (Washington, DC: Fall 1996); IFC, *World Bank Environmental Policy*, (Washington, DC: 17 April 1994); IFC, "Environmental Requirements for Project Sponsors," undated; Ronald Anderson, IFC, discussion with author, 29 June 1995; on Bank's shortcomings in implementing policies, see Leyla Boulton, "World Bank Admits to Weakness on Environment," *Financial Times*, 4 October 1996, and Mark Suzman, "World Bank Accuses Itself of 'Serious Violations'," *Financial Times*, 7 January 1998.

73. "A New Environmental Sensitivity at the World Bank," Highlights from World Bank President James Wolfensohn's Speech at a WRI Dinner in Washington, DC, *International Perspectives on Sustainability*, WRI, March 1996; James D. Wolfensohn, remarks to Bank Group Seminar for NGOs on Private Sector Development and the Role of the Bank Group, Washington, DC, 6 June 1996; Abid Aslam, "Romawas Development: World Bank Offers Chance to Comment on IFC Policies," Inter Press Service, 15 January 1998; Center for International Environmental Law and FOE-U.S., "Proposal for an Independent Review Panel for the International Finance Corporation/ Multilateral Investment Guarantee Agency," draft, 15 August 1997.

74. International Rivers Network, "World Bank Agency Challenged on Loan for Chilean Dam," press release (Berkeley, CA: 17 November 1995); Leslie Crawford, "Chile Dam Row Shows IFC's Problems with Projects," *Financial Times*, 8 August 1997.

75. PERC and FOE, op. cit. note 11; PERC and FOE, "OPIC and the Environment: The Real Story," information sheet (Washington, DC: April 1997).

76. OPIC environmental requirements from Bruce Rich, Environmental Defense Fund, "The Need for Harmonization of Environmental and Social Assessment Criteria for Bilateral Export Credit and Investment Insurance Agencies," memorandum to U.S. National Security Council, December 1996, and from Bruce Rich, discussion with author, 22 January 1998; Peter Busowski, "OPIC Case Against U.S. Firm in Indonesia Raises Question of Authority, Project Scope," *International Environment Reporter*, 29 November

1995; $60 billion from Robert Bryce, "Environment: Struck By A Golden Spear," *The Guardian* (London), 17 January 1996; Stewart Yerton, "Mine Venture: Battle Between Ecology, Profits," *The Plain Dealer* (Cleveland), 28 January 1996; Janine Robers, "UK Cash Props Up Terror Mine," *The Independent* (London), 26 November 1995.

77. "Business Brief—Freeport-McMoran Copper & Gold Inc.: Federal Agency Reinstates Insurance on Firm's Project," *Wall Street Journal*, 22 April 1996; "Freeport-McMoran Copper & Gold Cancels Government Policy," *Wall Street Journal*, 23 September 1996.

78. "President Clinton's Address to U.N. General Assembly Special Session, 26 June 1997," summary released by The White House; PERC and FOE, "President Announces Environmental Reforms for Public Finance Agencies; Groups Gratified but Not Satisfied," press release (Washington, DC: 26 June 1997).

79. John H. Cushman, "Ex-Im Bank Refuses Loan Backing for Big China Dam," *New York Times*, 31 May 1996; Tony Walker, "Power Hungry on the Gorges," *Financial Times*, 17 February 1997; Office of the Press Secretary, The White House, "Remarks by the President in Address to the United Nations Special Session on Environment and Development," 26 June 1997, Rich, "Need for Harmonization," op. cit. note 76; Summit of the Eight, "Communiqué," Denver, 22 June 1997.

80. Michelle Chan-Fishel, "Risk Exposure: Revealing Environmental and Political Risk to Private Financiers," draft report (Washington, DC: FOE, 11 May 1996); Gentry, op. cit. note 53; Stephan Schmidheiny and Federico J.L. Zorraquín, with the World Business Council for Sustainable Development, *Financing Change* (Cambridge, MA: The MIT Press, 1996); "Bankers Urged to Include Assessments of Environmental Risk in Lending Decisions," *International Environment Reporter*, 14 May 1997.

81. Gentry, op. cit. note 53; John T. Ganzi and Julie Tanner, "Global Survey on Environmental Policies and Practices of the Financial Services Industry: The Private Sector," sponsored by National Wildlife Federation, Washington, DC, produced by Environment & Finance Enterprise, 16 May 1997.

82. "UNEP's Third International Round Table Meeting," *Financial Services Initiative*, UNEP Newsletter, August 1997; United Nations Environment Programme (UNEP), "Bankers to Link Environment and Financial Performance," press release (New York: 16 May 1997); "Banking and the Environment, A Statement by Banks on the Environment and Sustainable Development," 1992, supplied by Deborah Vorhies, UNEP, Geneva; Julie Hill, Doreen Fedrigo, and Ingrid Marshall, *Banking on the Future, A Survey of Implementation of the UNEP Statement by Banks on Environment and Sustainable Development* (London: Green Alliance, March 1997).

83. Mark A. Cohen, Scott A. Fenn, and Jonathan S. Naimon, *Environmental and Financial Performance: Are They Related?* (Washington, DC: Investor

Responsibility Research Center (IRRC), April 1995); Stanley J. Feldman, Peter A. Soyka, and Paul Ameer, *Does Improving a Firm's Environmental Management System and Environmental Performance Result in a Higher Stock Price?* (Fairfax, VA: ICF Kaiser International, Inc., November 1996). See also Jerald Blumburg, Åge Korsvold, and Georges Blum, *Environmental Performance and Shareholder Value* (Geneva: World Business Council for Sustainable Development, undated), and "Environmentally Responsible Investments Outperform Others," *Business and the Environment*, July 1997.

84. "The Global Environment Fund Group," information sheet (Washington, DC: September 1996); Greg Nagler, Investment Analyst, Global Environment Fund, discussion with Payal Sampat, Worldwatch Institute, 30 October 1997.

85. Social Investment Forum, *Responsible Investing Trends in the United States* (Washington, DC: 1997); "Green Investing Picks Up Steam," *EHS Management*, 4 August 1997; Chan-Fishel, op. cit. note 80; "1996 SRI Industry Highlights & Changes," and "Mutual Fund Returns," *Green Money Journal*, spring 1997; Domini 400 Index from Peter Kinder, President, Kinder, Lydenberg and Domini Co., Inc. (KLD), discussion with Payal Sampat, Worldwatch Institute, 22 October 1997, and from KLD, "Domini 400 Social Index Gains 5.53% in September, S&P 500 Gains 5.45%," press release (Cambridge, MA: 17 October 1997).

86. Michelle Chan-Fishel, "International SRI," *GreenMoney Journal* online, <http://www.greenmoney.com/gmj/spr97/chan.htm>. For a list of socially responsible mutual funds, see the Social Investment Forum at <http://www.socialinvest.org/>; Patareeya Benjapolchai, Senior Vice President, the Stock Exchange of Thailand, "Stock Exchange Policies for Protecting the Environment," address to "The Environment and Financial Performance," UNEP's Third International Roundtable Meeting on Finance and the Environment," Columbia University, New York, 22-23 May 1997; Gentry, op. cit. note 53.

87. IFC, *Annual Report 1997* (Washington, DC: 1997).

88. World Bank, *Annual Report 1997*, op. cit. note 70; $15 million from Mark Constantine, Manager of Corporate Relations, IFC, discussion with Payal Sampat, Worldwatch Institute, 23 October 1997; small loans from "EEAF Investments up to February, 1997," information sheet (Arlington, VA: Environmental Enterprises Assistance Fund, Inc., 1997).

89. World Bank, *Annual Report 1997*, op. cit. note 70; World Bank, "Private Sector Information Kiosk," from <http://www.worldbank.org/html/gef/private/priv.htm>, viewed 17 September 1997; Douglas Salloum, Small and Medium Enterprises Program Manager, IFC, discussion with Payal Sampat, Worldwatch Institute, 29 October 1997; IFC, op. cit. note 87; Alex Wilks, "The World Bank's Promotion of Privatisation and Private Sector Development: Issues and Concerns," Bretton Woods Project, London, February 1997.

90. See, for example, "The World Economy: The Future of the State," *The Economist*, 20 September 1997, and Peter F. Drucker, "The Global Economy and the Nation-State," *Foreign Affairs*, September/October 1997; World Bank, *Five Years after Rio: Innovations in Environmental Policy* (Washington, DC: 1997); David Malin Roodman, *Paying the Piper: Subsidies, Politics, and the Environment*, Worldwatch Paper 133 (Washington, DC: Worldwatch Institute, December 1996); David Malin Roodman, *Getting the Signals Right: Tax Reform to Protect the Environment and the Economy* (Washington, DC: Worldwatch Institute, May 1997).

91. World Bank, op. cit. note 90.

92. Schmidheiny and Zorraquín, op. cit. note 80; IRRC, "Environmental Disclosure at S & P 500 Companies' Non-U.S. Operations," press release (Washington, DC: 1 December 1997).

93. Benjapolchai, op. cit. note 86.

94. Concerns about international competitiveness have been voiced loudly in the debate in the United States about the Kyoto Protocol to the climate treaty, as well as in earlier debates in both the European Union and the United States about proposed carbon and energy taxes. Although these arguments do not generally hold up to close scrutiny, they nonetheless exert a strong pull in the policy arena. For a fuller discussion of these issues, see Robert Repetto, *Jobs, Competitiveness, and Environmental Regulation: What Are The Real Issues* (Washington, DC: WRI, March 1995); Robert Repetto and Crescencia Maurer, with Garren C. Bird, "U.S. Competitiveness Is Not at Risk in the Climate Negotiations," WRI Climate Protection Initiative, Climate Notes, October 1997; J. Andrew Hoerner and Frank Muller, "The Impact of a Broad-Based Energy Tax on the Competitiveness of U.S. Industry," *Tax Notes*, 21 June 1993; and Daniel C. Esty and Bradford S. Gentry, "Foreign Investment, Globalisation, and Environment," in OECD, *Globalisation and the Environment: Preliminary Perspectives* (Paris: 1997).

95. Tony Jackson, "Facing Up to a Challenging Opposition," *Financial Times*, 31 October 1997; Schmidheiny and Zorraquín, op. cit. note 80; UNCTAD, *Self Regulation of Environmental Management: An Analysis of Guidelines Set by International Industry Associations for Their Member Firms* (New York: United Nations, 1996); Control Risks Group, *No Hiding Place: Business and the Politics of Pressure* (London: July 1997); "Lawyers See Rise in Court Cases Attempting to Apply U.S. Laws Outside Borders," *International Environment Reporter*, 25 June 1997.

96. On International Organization for Standardization (ISO) certification see, for example, "Certification under ISO 14001 Expected for a Dozen Thai Firms in 1997," *International Environment Reporter*, 16 April 1997, "Czech Chemical Firm First to be Certified under 14001 in Former Eastern Bloc Country," *International Environment Reporter*, 5 March 1997, and "Environmental Management Systems: ISO Standard 14000," *International Environment Reporter*,

7 August 1996; "ISO 14001, 14004 Standards Finalized; U.K. To Withdraw Its Measure in March," *International Environment Reporter*, 2 October 1996; Benchmark Environmental Consulting, "ISO 14001: An Uncommon Perspective," Portland, ME, November 1995, reprinted February 1996, <http://www.envirocom.com:80/standards/iso/14001/info.htm>, viewed 10 February 1997; "ISO 14024 Eco-Labeling Proposal Posed to Become Draft International Standard," *International Environment Reporter*, 3 September 1997; "Life Cycle Analysis Committee Gives Future ISO Standard a Push Forward," *International Environment Reporter*, 30 April 1997.

97. Pierre Hauselmann, *ISO Inside Out: ISO and Environmental Management*, WWF International Discussion Paper (Gland, Switzerland: June 1996).

98. "North American Agreement on Environmental Cooperation, 1993," in *NAFTA Supplemental Agreements* (Washington, DC: U.S. Government Printing Office, 1993); Daniel Magraw, "NAFTA's Repercussions: Is Green Trade Possible?" *Environment*, March 1994.

99. Environmental benefits of NAFTA listed in U.S. Government, *Study on the Operation and Effects of the North American Free Trade Agreement*, 1997, <http://www.ustr.gov/reports/index.html>, viewed 8 October 1997; for an independent assessment, see Justin R. Ward, *The Greening of North American Trade, Four Years Later: A Summary and Report Card on Implementation of the NAFTA Environmental Package* (Washington, DC: Natural Resources Defense Council, 10 September 1997); 44 tons from Alberto Bustani, "Environmental Needs and Infrastructure in Mexico," 21 April 1995, cited in David W. Eaton, "NAFTA and the Environment; A Proposal for Free Trade in Hazardous Waste Between the United States and Mexico," *St. Mary's Law Journal*, no.4, 1996.

100. Molly O'Meara, "Riding the Dragon," *World Watch*, March/April 1997; Asia-Pacific Economic Cooperation, *Implementing the APEC Vision*, Third Report of the Eminent Persons Group (Singapore: August 1995).

101. WWF, *The OECD Multilateral Agreement on Investment*, WWF International Briefing (Gland, Switzerland: March 1997); FOE, "The OECD Multilateral Agreement on Investment (MAI): Examples of Laws that Would Conflict with the MAI," <http://www.foe.org/ga/exshort.html>, viewed 23 October 1997; Mark Vallianatos, FOE, "Update on Negotiations for a Multilateral Investment Agreement," memo to international activists (Washington, DC: 4 August 1997); International Non-Governmental Organisations, "Global Investment Treaty Challenged by International Coalition of NGOs," press release, 27 October 1997, <csdgen@nygate.undp.org>, viewed 24 October 1997; International Institute for Sustainable Development, (IISD), "WTO Ministerial Conference, 9-13 December 1996," *Sustainable Developments*, no. 6, 1996.

102. "The OECD Multilateral Agreement on Investment: Examples of Laws," op. cit. note 101.

103. Jeffrey Sachs, "IMF Is a Power unto Itself," *Financial Times*, 11 December 1997; David Reed, ed., *Structural Adjustment, the Environment, and Sustainable Development* (London: Earthscan Publications, Ltd., 1996).

104. Reed, op. cit. note 103; "IMF Decides Once Again to Halt Disbursement of Loans because of Illegal Timber Practices," *International Environment Reporter*, 15 October 1997; Alassane D. Ouattara, Deputy Managing Director, IMF, Address at the World Bank's Fifth Annual Conference on Environmentally and Socially Sustainable Development, Washington, DC, 7 October 1997.

105. Conventions on biological diversity and climate change included in Lakshman D. Guruswamy, Sir Geoffrey W. R. Palmer, and Burns H. Weston, *International Environmental Law and World Order*, Supplement of Basic Documents (St. Paul, MN: West Publishing Co., 1994); biodiversity treaty ratifications from Convention on Biological Diversity secretariat, <http://www.biodiv.org/conv/ratify.html>, viewed 26 January 1998; role of biodiversity treaty from John Fitzgerald, independent attorney, discussion with author, 23 October 1997; climate treaty ratifications from IISD, "Report of the Third Conference of the Parties to the United Nations Framework Convention on Climate Change: 1-11 December 1997," *Earth Negotiations Bulletin*, 13 December 1997; "Final Kyoto Protocol to the U.N. Framework Convention on Climate Change, Including Annex of Participating Countries, Commitments, Approved December 11, 1997," reproduced in *International Environment Reporter*, 7 January 1998.

106. Influence of World Bank guidelines from "Attorney Says Environmental Trends Abroad Will Have Far-Reaching Impact on U.S. Firms," *International Environment Reporter*, 1 November 1995; UNEP sectoral task forces described in "UNEP's Past Two Years; A Period of Significant Accomplishments," information sheet (New York: UNEP, May 1997).

107. Jeff Gerth, "Where Business Rules: Forging Global Regulations That Put Industry First," *New York Times*, 9 January 1998; Smitu Kothari, "Rising from the Margins: The Awakening of Civil Society in the Third World," *Development*, no. 3, 1996; Jonathan Friedland, "Across Latin America, New Environmentalists Extend Their Reach," *Wall Street Journal*, 26 March 1997; "'Green' Groups Cheer Venezuelan Gold Ruling," *Journal of Commerce*, 13 November 1997.

108. Control Risks Group, op. cit. note 95; Lisa Jordan (Bank Information Center, Washington, DC) and Peter van Tuijl (Consultant, Novib, Amsterdam, Netherlands), "Political Responsibility in NGO Advocacy: Exploring Emerging Shapes of Global Democracy," unpublished paper, June 1997; Chan, op. cit. note 69; Leyla Boulton, "Activists Take Up Sharper Arrows," *Financial Times*, 13 May 1997.

109. Jackson, op. cit. note 95; Control Risks Group, op. cit. note 95; Control Risks Group description from <http://www.crg.com/ControlRisks/crg/index.html>, viewed 13 October 1997.

Worldwatch Papers

No. of Copies

Worldwatch Papers by Hilary F. French

_____**Total copies (transfer number to order form on next page)**

PUBLICATION ORDER FORM

_____ *State of the World:* $13.95
The annual book used by journalists, activists, scholars, and policymakers
worldwide to get a clear picture of the environmental problems we face.

_____ **Worldwatch Library: $30.00 (international subscribers $45)**
Receive *State of the World* and all six Worldwatch Papers as they are released
during the calendar year.

_____ *Vital Signs:* $12.00
The book of trends that are shaping our future in easy to read graph and table
format, with a brief commentary on each trend.

_____ **WORLD WATCH magazine subscription: $20.00 (international airmail $35.00)**
Stay abreast of global environmental trends and issues with our award-winning,
eminently readable bimonthly magazine.

_____ **Worldwatch Database Disk Subscription: $89.00**
Contains global agricultural, energy, economic, environmental, social, and
military indicators from all current Worldwatch publications including this Paper.
Includes a mid-year update, and *Vital Signs* and *State of the World* as they are
published. Can be used with Lotus 1-2-3, Quattro Pro, Excel, SuperCalc and
many other spreadsheets.
Check one: _____ **IBM-compatible** _____ **Macintosh**

_____ **Worldwatch Papers—See list on previous page**
Single copy: $5.00 • 2–5: $4.00 ea. • 6–20: $3.00 ea. • 21 or more:
$2.00 ea. (Call Vice President for Communications at (202) 452-1999
for discounts on larger orders.)

$4.00* Shipping and Handling *($8.00 outside North America)*

_____ **TOTAL** (U.S. dollars only)
minimum charge for S&H; call (800) 555-2028 for bulk order S&H

Make check payable to Worldwatch Institute
1776 Massachusetts Ave., NW, Washington, DC 20036-1904 USA

Enclosed is my check or purchase order for U.S. $_____

☐ AMEX ☐ VISA ☐ MasterCard _____
                                  Card Number   Expiration Date

name   **daytime phone #**

address

city   **state**   **zip/country**

phone: (202) 452-1999   fax: (202) 296-7365   e-mail: wwpub@worldwatch.org
website: www.worldwatch.org

Wish to make a tax-deductible contribution? Contact Worldwatch to find out how
your donation can help advance our work.